You don't need an MBA to put these great ideas to
understands the theoretical nuances of financial ma
way that is powerfully practical. The chapter that deals with seven key biblical principles
that should serve as the foundation for school finance is worth the price of the book.

Steve Whitaker, EdD
Headmaster, The First Academy
Orlando, FL

A must-read for Christian school administrators desiring to establish responsible, God-
honoring financial management. In engaging and convincing fashion, Dr. Pue addresses
the gamut of fiscal issues facing Christian school leaders. From a foundation of nonnegotiable biblical principles to policies and practices for budgeting, setting tuition rates and
compensation levels, and resource procurement, he offers readers a plethora of practical
insights for strategic money management particularly relevant for twenty-first-century
Christian education institutions.

Gordon B. Brown, EdD
Visiting Professor, Columbia International University
Columbia, SC

"Thanks, I needed that!" Like the old slap-in-the-face aftershave commercial, Alan is calling us to take a hard look in our financial mirror, while giving us a timely (but loving) cuff
across our administrative head. Through his veteran insight and experience, he has related
a number of key principles, and confirmed one ... that the pain of not changing is growing
greater than the pain of change. Bravo!

Bill Stevens
Head of School, Wilmington Christian School
Hockessin, DE

Far too often, Christian school administrators find themselves fixated on important spiritual or educational matters and may ignore the need to manage finances with excellence
as well. Alan Pue's book calls school leaders to a more balanced perspective. His relentless commitment to biblical principles and an utterly realistic budgeting process should
encourage even the most experienced administrator. The section on the value of the budget
emerging from a strategic planning process is worth the price of the book. I highly recommend this resource for all Christian school leaders.

Sherry Worel
Superintendent, Stoneybrooke Christian Schools
San Juan Capistrano, CA

Have you ever wanted to have a conversation with a financial advisor but couldn't find one who understood your ministry and concerns? Your search is over! Alan Pue coaches his readers with the voice of a seasoned veteran on crucial financial topics such as budgeting, board responsibilities, and strategic planning concepts. This text is well researched, contains a strong biblical underpinning, and is written in an entertaining style. His readers will recognize that Dr. Pue has successfully led a Christian school and understands all aspects of a ministry's operation.

Dr. Ken Coley
Author and former administrator
Wake Forest, NC

Dr. Alan Pue's book on school finances is a welcome contribution to the Christian school movement. His insight, wisdom, and experience are evident in his development of this timely and critical topic. He blends relevant issues, biblical positioning, and practical implications in such a way that the reader is encouraged to rethink and retool for God-honoring school financial sustainability. This book is worthy of consideration—and most importantly, application—by administrators and boards of all Christian schools.

Dr. Sandy M. Outlar
Liaison to Christian Schools
Lancaster Bible College
Lancaster, PA

Alan Pue brings insights from Scripture, current management literature, and a lifetime of ministry experience to this concise analysis of Christian school finance. As a pastor, head of a Christian school, Christian college administrator, and consultant, he has lived "in the trenches" and has dealt with these issues in multiple settings. What separates this book from others is the integration of foundational principles with practical suggestions. We expect books on finance to discuss budgets, spreadsheets, revenue, expense, etc. In addition to practical insights on those traditional topics, this book connects mission, leadership, excellence, and trust to finance. There is invaluable help for young schools and new administrators as well as valuable insights for established schools and veteran administrators. A thoughtful treatment of Christian school finance has long been needed. Alan Pue has filled that void with a thoroughly biblical call for excellence in financial management for Christian schools.

Stephen P. Dill, EdD
Head of School
Delaware County Christian School
Newtown Square, PA

Rethinking
Sustainability

Rethinking
Sustainability

A Strategic Financial Model for Christian Schools

Alan Pue

purposeful design®
p u b l i c a t i o n s

Colorado Springs, Colorado

© 2012 by Alan Pue

Purposeful Design Publications is the publishing division of the Association of Christian Schools International (ACSI) and is committed to the ministry of Christian school education, to enable Christian educators and schools worldwide to effectively prepare students for life. As the publisher of textbooks, trade books, and other educational resources within ACSI, Purposeful Design Publications strives to produce biblically sound materials that reflect Christian scholarship and stewardship and that address the identified needs of Christian schools around the world.

The views expressed in this publication are those of the author, and they may not necessarily represent the position of the Association of Christian Schools International.

Scripture quotations marked NIV are taken from the Holy Bible, NEW INTERNATIONAL VERSION®. Copyright © 1973, 1978, 1984 by International Bible Society. All rights reserved worldwide. Used by permission of Biblica, Inc.

Scripture quotations marked KJV are taken from the King James Version.

Scripture quotations marked ESV are taken from the Holy Bible, English Standard Version. Copyright © 2001 by Crossway Bibles, a division of Good News Publishers.

Scripture quotations marked NASB are taken from the New American Standard Bible˚, Copyright © 1960, 1962, 1963, 1968, 1971, 1972, 1973, 1975, 1977, 1995 by The Lockman Foundation. Used by permission.

Printed in the United States of America
18 17 16 15 14 13 12   1 2 3 4 5 6 7

Pue, Alan
  Rethinking sustainability: A strategic financial model for Christian schools
  ISBN 978-1-58331-393-0 Catalog #6519

Design team: Mike Riester, Bethany Kerstetter
Editorial team: Christina Reidl, John Conaway, Gina Brandon

Purposeful Design Publications
A Division of ACSI
PO Box 65130 • Colorado Springs, CO 80962-5130
Customer Service: 800-367-0798 • www.acsi.org

Dedication

It is popular today to speak of life as a journey. If that is the case, my journey has taken enough detours and side roads to make a trip down Route 66 look boring in comparison. At the end of this book, I identify many of the people who have played a significant role in helping me navigate the many unexpected turns along that journey and who have enriched my life in the process.

There is one person, though, to whom I would like to dedicate this book. Babe, this is for you. You have traveled with me every step of the way. This doesn't happen if not for your enduring love; timely, gracious encouragement; and infinite patience. I don't know anyone else who could have or would have stuck by my side through it all. Thanks.

Contents

Foreword

I met Alan Pue in the spring of 1994. He was a Christian school consultant with GrowthMasters, located in Colorado Springs, and I was executive director of the Institute for Christian School Development (ICSD), located in Woodland Park, Colorado. Both GrowthMasters and the Institute were strategically involved with the Association of Christian Schools International (ACSI). Dr. Paul Kienel, then President of ACSI, suggested that ICSD and GrowthMasters consider merging in order to better serve the needs of the growing Christian school movement.

Alan and I spent hours together talking about the needs of schools, the pressures on administrators, and what could be done to bring encouragement and hope to the Christian school movement. These discussions were exciting. Alan and I realized that we shared a passion for the cause of Christian schooling and that we could learn from each other. These discussions led to the creation of SchoolMasters, a division of GrowthMasters.

Alan Pue is an idea generator. He can articulate a problem, put that problem in a philosophical context, and anticipate the effects of potential solutions. He stimulates brainstorming and creative thinking. In those days I was much more of an idea implementer. Alan would offer the philosophical, which would stimulate me to offer a strategy or a step-by-step approach. We fed off each other.

SchoolMasters served hundreds of Christian schools by offering strategic planning, funding, fund-raising, board training, professional development for faculty, and personal coaching for school leaders. We developed several models that are still being used by hundreds of schools around the world.

Alan taught me a great deal about problem solving. Because of his influence, I am much better at seeing the context of a problem and the implications of various potential solutions.

In this book, Alan Pue tackles the difficult, critical task of strategic finance for Christian schools. He develops his thesis with the same wisdom, insight, courage, and innovation that have made him such a valuable colleague, collaborator, and partner in this ministry of Christian schooling.

I would use three words to describe this book: *biblical, comprehensive,* and *strategic.* All three qualities are needed in order to appropriately address the complex issue of Christian school finances.

Biblical truth permeates the principles, concepts, and themes in this book. Alan is a keen student of God's Word, and that quality is evident. Alan has developed an excellent manifesto that all Christian educators will find practical and distinctively Christ-honoring. This book is a manual—a how-to, why-to, and when-to—designed to help Christian school leaders in the areas of budgeting and financial management.

This book is comprehensive enough to deal appropriately with the myriad of considerations involved in formulating financial plans and procedures. I am grateful for Alan's ability to contextualize concepts and principles that connect the realities of principle and practice. He writes from the perspective of an experienced Christian school head and a consultant for hundreds of Christian organizations. He has gained a depth of knowledge and insight from working with a broad variety of structures, governances, and types of Christian organizations. Out of this background, he has created a treatise on the essential ingredients of financial management.

Finally, this book is strategic. Because the book is biblical and comprehensive, it is purposeful. Alan calls us to develop strategic plans, procedures, and practices to address matters absolutely critical to the advance of God's kingdom—and then develop financial procedures and practices that reflect the strategic direction of the school.

This book could very well be one of the most important works you can study as you face the tremendous tasks of budget development and financial management of your Christian school.

Mickey Bowdon
Vice President for Christian School Education, Columbia International University
Headmaster, Ben Lippen School
Columbia, SC

Foreword

Dr. Alan Pue has written an important book about Christian school finances that needs to be read in its historical context, which I offer in brief.

I remember Alan Pue's arrival at an early version of what today is known as The PAIDEIA Conference, held that year at Eastern University, near Philadelphia. The purpose of this conference, from its beginning in 1984, has always been the same: "Strengthening the financial base of the Christian school." He came to this event as someone who had grown up attending a church-sponsored Christian school in Florida. After college, he had returned to his school to teach and coach and offer guidance before going on to other ministry. He came to that conference as the only active pastor-and-headmaster in the group; he was also demonstrably the best golfer, as the rest of us duffers learned during our conference outing.

I had been offering counsel to schools and colleges since 1965, when The College Board appointed me as its first consultant on the Advanced Placement Program. But in 1974, I returned from a global tour of Christian schools convinced that, while Christian schooling certainly needed a healthy dose of improved academic rigor such as the AP Program offered, Christian schooling also needed to overhaul its standard financial model. That model was based on what I began calling "The Post-Depression Syndrome"; it infected most of us who had lived through and barely survived the 1930s' financial Slough of Despond. The principle that lingered in the souls of many Christian school leaders in the 1970s and 1980s—godly men and women who had been scared and scarred by their own childhood privation—was based on an economic theory whose key word was *cheap*. The mantra for running a typical Christian school was "Keep the tuition as low as possible."

This was not merely a call for thrift and the avoidance of wasteful luxury and lavish excess; it was primarily a call to accept being "cheap and clean for Jesus!" There was something supposedly more "godly" about being frayed and tawdry rather than bright and attractive. In fact, such "godliness" could almost be measured by what Christian schools did not possess in the way of current technology and did not offer in programs or paychecks. In order to limit the cost of a Christian school's operations, its board members needed the cooperation and complicity of their head, administrators, and teachers (who would work for subpoverty wages) and of parents who would settle for mediocre-to-inferior facilities and instruction for their children in order to avoid paying a higher rate of tuition. Of course, there were notable exceptions to this generalization—schools whose founders had a higher vision, heads and teachers who excelled in spite of hardship. But the general state of Christian schooling during the boom years of the 70s and 80s was financially naïve and utterly opposed to tolerating any "worldly" nexus between *mission* and *money.*

For more than two decades, the message my consulting colleagues and I tried to propagate went largely unheard, until 1996, when Ken Smitherman, former president of ACSI, endorsed the publishing of *From Candy Sales to Committed Donors: A Guide to Financing Christian Schools.* In fact, I later learned, I was considered in some high circles to be nothing more than a materialistic huckster and rabble-rouser against the status quo. And just what was that oh-so-radical message? We called upon school boards and their heads to *fund the mission fully.* We believed that, in recognition of an economic reality called "the cost of doing business," the subtext to the key words of a school's mission statement ought to be dollar signs and specific amounts to be expended on achieving that school's reason-for-being—or else stop promising *excellence* you don't intend to provide!

Some of you representing the current generation of Christian school leaders—those who have come to maturity and responsibility in the twenty-first century—may mistake what I have been describing for "stranger than fiction." Not, however, if you yourself were a student in a Christian school in that era, in which case, it's all too familiar in your memory, even though you had no part in those financial decisions.

As Pue tells us in the preface and early chapters that follow, this was the environment from which he came as a young pastor and school founder from Delaware. At The PAIDEIA Conference he entered a new country and heard a different language: *value-based tuition* instead of "tuition as low as possible"; *need-based financial aid,* not discounts for every unthinkable reason; *voluntary gift support* in place of product sales and fund-raising events; and so on. I recall that he was both friendly and wary: friendly because that's his nature, wary because he had probably been warned against the heresy he would hear at our conference.

But he absorbed the new counsel he heard, sifted and weighed it, used what made sense to him, adapted and refined what needed to be altered. He did so because this is a man who—long ago—learned to think for himself and to think in the context of biblical truth rather than conventional dogma. As you will see throughout the pages of this book, Dr. Pue is steeped in the truth of God's Word and is not afraid to unpack some of its more difficult and disturbing passages and address the questions they raise.

For me, the best synopsis of Alan Pue's intention in writing this book can be found in a single paragraph on page 110: "These questions are important. The answer is simple. Every head of school bears the responsibility for determining the cost of providing an education that fully achieves the school's mission with excellence and integrity. To do otherwise is to dishonor God and disregard the promises the school has made to its parents, students, teachers, and community."

Over the years of our friendship, Alan Pue has developed into a respected adviser to boards and heads of Christian schools. Working under the identity of The Barnabas Group, he recalls my own favorite figure in the early church. The apostles and deacons gave Joseph of Cyprus the nickname Barnabas, meaning "son of encouragement" (Acts 4:36, NIV). What better recommendation for a consultant than to be known as someone who encourages others!

D. Bruce Lockerbie
Chairman, PAIDEIA, Inc.
Stony Brook, NY

Preface

Budgeting and financial management are difficult tasks even for the most well-prepared, capable person. It isn't a game for amateurs; the potential negative consequences are simply too great. And even when professionals are involved, if you approach the task from a set of flawed assumptions, you are still likely to end up in the proverbial ditch or (more to the point) out of business.

Now here is the reality. Most of us called to Christian school leadership came to our task of creating and managing the financial resources of our schools wholly unprepared. Indeed, we are often bewildered and over-whelmed by the responsibility, and in desperation and ignorance we end up adopting practices based on all kinds of false assumptions that usually make the problem worse. The result is enormous personal angst and frustration, a continuing struggle for survival or worse, and great harm to the cause of Christian schooling.

I know that scenario well. I've lived it. Only by God's grace and the wisdom and practical insight of one man, Dr. Bruce Lockerbie, was I able to escape the prison of so much flawed thinking and practice. I say by God's grace, because I just "happened" to stumble into one of Dr. Lockerbie's workshops at a school conference in Pennsylvania. He challenged all my assumptions about financing a Christian school. I must confess I didn't immediately adopt what he was saying. In fact I was resistant to much of what he taught that day.

I knew this, however. As a school we were in trouble—serious trouble. I knew if we didn't start doing things differently, our future was in question. So I asked questions, put new practices into place over time, and prayed—a lot. Improvement in our financial situation didn't become apparent im-mediately, but the trajectory began to change significantly. My financial education didn't happen overnight. And even today, more than a quarter of a century later, it isn't complete. For example, at this moment I am learning all I can about estate planning and planned gifts because I believe they will be key in building a sustainable future for Christian schools.

A few years ago Dr. Bob Miller of the Association of Christian Schools International (ACSI) asked me to develop a one-day workshop on school finance, what ACSI calls an enabler. I agreed to his request and began piecing together material from a variety of sources. Sadly, I discovered little in the marketplace on the topic of Christian school finance. Oh, there are many books on how to construct a budget. Some of those are even written with nonprofit organizations in mind. What was lacking, however, was a comprehensive, integrated look at this topic written specifically for the leaders of Christian schools.

The purpose of this book is to address that vacuum. I am certain there are others who could do a better job. But I'm tired of waiting. The need is too great. In a way I'm still an amateur myself. I am, however, a scarred, grizzled veteran of budgeting wars who decided long ago that there had to be a better way.

Before you plunge into the heart of what I have to say, permit me three brief observations.

First, please understand that this is not intended to be the definitive work on Christian school budgeting. I'm not a CPA. This is budgeting 101, not a graduate symposium. What I have tried to do is provide a holistic look at the whys and hows of budgeting in a Christian school. Indeed, you may already utilize a sound budgeting system, but it is imperative to understand that even with the finest software you can only manipulate the numbers you input. Without a sound set of principles and appropriate assumptions, all you will do in the end is effectively manage flawed numbers.

So second, it is my goal to lay a proper foundation upon which you can build a sound budget and budgeting process. Thus in chapters 1 through 6 it is my goal to identify and explore key biblical and budgeting principles. In so doing it is likely that I will touch on one or more of your sacred cows. But as someone long ago noted, "Sacred cows make the best hamburger." It is not my goal in this section to be simply provocative. However, it is my goal to draw attention to some ideas that we in the Christian school movement have tended to ignore, and to challenge some firmly held beliefs that I think have contributed to the current financial challenges so many Christian schools experience.

Finally, it is my goal to provide a sound framework for thinking about the budgeting process, both the expense side of that process and the income side. In chapters 7 through 14, I will touch on such questions as these:

- What is a cost-center-based budget, and why does that matter?
- Who should be involved in the budgeting process, and how?
- How do you connect your long-term vision for your school to current operational realities?
- From what resources do you generate the revenue necessary to fund your mission and vision?
- What keeps you from achieving the fiscal health you so desire for your school?

Here is the challenging reality. Christian schools all over the United States and around the world share one thing in common: they are underfunded and overwhelmed as a direct consequence of poor fiscal-management and resource-development practice. It is my passionate desire that reading this book will launch you on a journey toward a better understanding of school financial practice and thus greater health and long-term sustainability.

Reading this book, however, is just a first step for you, your leadership team, and your board. Next you will need to act. It is my prayer that you will have the courage to do what needs to be done to build a sound financial foundation for the school you have been called to lead.

Castle Rock, Colorado
March 22, 2012

Chapter One
It Is Now or Maybe Never

Why does this book matter? The answer is simple. It's because your school matters. A lot. The world needs strong Christian schools. Yet my own anecdotal observations and research done by the Association of Christian Schools International (ACSI) reveal that financial uncertainty and weakness continue to plague Christian schools, putting far too many of them at risk.

Now a second set of questions: Why do Christian schools matter? What is lost if a Christian school or even a significant number of Christian schools go out of business? Are Christian schools really crucial to our future, or are they just a nice alternative for those families able to afford the tuition? These are fair questions, ones you must answer well if you expect to build strong, long-term support for your school.

While answering these particular questions is not the primary purpose of this book, I happen to believe that Christian schools are much more than a nice alternative to the public school down the street. I believe that Christian schooling is a biblical mandate and that Christian schools are our best hope for producing a generation of disciples who can change their world, a world that is increasingly complex and indifferent to the message of the gospel. I also believe, however, that the enterprise of Christian schooling will remain at risk until, and unless, Christian school leaders and supporters begin to think more strategically about how to best fund Christian schools.

How important are our schools? Let's take a brief look at our current reality.

Turbulent Times

In a conversation with Peter Drucker recorded by Ken Blanchard in his book *Mission Possible*, Drucker, considered by many to be the most insightful organizational expert of the twentieth century, observed, "Every few hundred years throughout Western history, a sharp transformation has occurred. In a matter of decades, society altogether rearranges itself—its world view, its basic values, its social and political structures, its arts, its key institutions. Fifty years later a new world exists. And the people born into that world cannot even imagine the world in which grandparents lived and into which their own parents were born" (1997, 82).

I doubt that many of you would disagree that we live in just such an era. As a baby boomer in his sixth decade, I am confident that we live in the time that Drucker describes. My grandchildren will know nothing of life without the World Wide Web, cell phones, iPods, and instant messaging. They are not computer geeks but rather *digital natives*, a term that describes those who have grown up in a world filled with computers, cell phones, and cable TV. They will grow to adulthood drenched in a cascading, virtually inescapable series of images and messages, each carefully constructed to sell a particular product or idea. The impact is unmistakable.

In his book *The Last Christian Generation*, Josh McDowell writes, "I realize the title of this book may be shocking. But the decision to call this *The Last Christian Generation* was not made lightly nor was it done for sensationalism. I sincerely believe unless something is done now to change the spiritual state of our young people—*you* will become the last Christian generation!" (2006, 11; italics in original). McDowell goes on to reveal the disconcerting results of some significant research into the minds of the millennial generation. He writes, "Today's youth seem to be just as interested in God and just as passionate about spiritual things as any generation…. Their interest is not in question at all. But the fundamental question is: 'How are they forming their view of God?' And what brand of religion are they adopting?" (15).

McDowell then gives some startling facts about young people. For example, 63 percent don't believe that Jesus is God's one true Son, 58 percent believe that all faiths teach equally valid truths, 51 percent don't believe that Jesus rose from the dead, 65 percent don't believe that Satan is a real entity, and 68 percent don't believe the Holy Spirit is a real entity. He then observes, "It's not that they haven't embraced a version of Christianity; it's simply that the version they believe in is not built on the true foundation of what biblical Christianity is all about" (2006, 15).

How can these startling findings be true? How can our kids be so wrong about such fundamental truths? How can they embrace God and spirituality and yet hold such profoundly wrong beliefs? In answer to that question, McDowell writes, "In the absence of foundational training, our young people have been influenced by a philosophy that permeates much of our society—government, schools, movies, television, and music—and guides much of their behaviors without them (or most of us) even being aware of it" (2006, 43).

Reread that quotation. Then focus on the phrase "in the absence of foundational training." I would argue that the foundational training to which McDowell refers can best take place in Christian schools. It's not that I think the church unconcerned or even incapable. And I would not even argue that every Christian school does a good job of equipping our young people to think and act Christianly. I would make the case, however, that Christian schooling, properly done, does provide the best context for the kind of in-depth discipling demonstrated in the Scriptures. However, poor financial health threatens the very survival of many Christian schools. If Christian schools cannot solve this problem, I fear we may very well face the reality of Josh McDowell's prediction.

A Collapse and a Response

Many of us who attended school in the 1950s remember learning to huddle under our desks as part of civil-defense drills in preparation for the unthinkable: nuclear war. Our generation could hardly imagine the events of 1989, when the wall between the free world and the bulk of the Communist world collapsed. The conflict that had shaped our generation seemed irresolvable. Then there on our television screens the citizens of both East and West Berlin were tearing down the wall that had separated families and symbolized a tyranny that had enslaved millions of people for much of the twentieth century.

Suddenly a world virtually closed to the gospel opened. The need was overwhelming and immediate, the obstacles were daunting, and (frankly) the church was not poised to respond in a strategic, focused manner. That situation could easily have descended into conflicting, highly parochial efforts in which the church could have invested and squandered enormous amounts of money for little impact.

Fortunately, that negative scenario, by and large, did not occur. In a rare but refreshing effort, major mission organizations worked together in a remarkable display of unity that resulted in a strategic, cooperative, and highly effective effort to plant new churches, share the gospel, and assist what had been for decades a persecuted underground church. Many of you probably had the privilege to participate in short-term ministry trips and to see firsthand what can take place when God's people work together to solve a difficult problem or to pursue a remarkable opportunity.

I believe we need that kind of united effort if we are going to reverse the decline in our culture. We need strong churches working together with strong Christian schools to maximize our distinct but complementary gifts in a genuine strategic partnership. Unfortunately, that united effort remains, at this point, an unrealized dream.

At present, Christian schools and local churches exist as wary allies at best. Each tends to view the other as a competitor rather than a partner. Many Christian schools have contributed to this perception by presenting themselves as organizations in need of constant support. Most of the time when we approach a pastor, we request help. We need money. We need access to the congregation. We need the pastor to promote our school. We need a good deal on renting the church's facilities. We need, we need, we need. This scenario does not show our position as one of strength.

Pastors for their part simply do not understand Christian schooling. Their study of theology did not include a category called education. Most of them do not easily make the connection between the purpose of the church and the purpose of Christian schools. Typically they think, "You teach kids to read, write, and compute. We teach kids to know God, to pray, and to share their faith. You are preparing kids for a career; we are preparing kids for the Kingdom." People tenaciously believe this false distinction.

How Then Should You Respond?

How can you best respond? How can you develop a strategic partnership that can fully and effectively respond to the crisis facing our young people today? I believe that you can take three crucial first steps.

First of all, you must help shift the paradigm through which most pastors view education. Until you change the way they think, you will find it difficult if not impossible to change the way they behave. To accomplish that goal, you must patiently cultivate deepening personal relationships with local pastors. And you cannot build such relationships in group meetings. You will need to make a significant investment of time. You simply cannot find a substitute for times of unhurried conversation. You may protest, "But I don't have that kind of time, and I don't know many pastors who do." Find a way, because we will face the reality of McDowell's book title if you don't.

Changing the way pastors think will require more than relationship, however. Second, you must also capture their imagination. In a recent e-mail, a dear friend who serves as a missionary in Brazil reminded me of an important fact. He wrote, "Statistical evidence, philosophical positioning, and cultural necessity are all relevant issues, but one of the most powerful ways to communicate a complex truth is through the use of metaphors." We need to capture not only the mind but the heart and imagination of pastors, and we are unlikely to do that through endless, unrelenting discussions on the true meaning and application of Deuteronomy chapter 6. Sometimes a simple metaphor will do the job of a thousand words.

Third, you must do at least one more thing, and therein lies the theme of this book. You must present your school as a strong partner that possesses significant resources to invest in the common cause of making disciples. Your school must not be viewed as weak or dependent, but at present I fear that most church leaders view you that way. That perception will not change, however, until your school becomes fiscally sound and until you demonstrate a strategic understanding of how to fund and deliver—with excellence—Christian schooling.

This book, therefore, is not just a how-to on building a budget. Don't get me wrong. Your school will never achieve fiscal health until you understand and implement good budgeting principles and practices. But you must comprehend more—much more—if you are going to create a fiscally sound school that has a foundation for the future. What role, for example, does wise planning or exceptional practice or sound systems or quality leadership play in creating a strong school? Each is important; you cannot ignore any without serious consequences. *Everything is connected.*

In focusing on sustainable schools, I hope to help you understand the comprehensive and integrated nature of funding. I hope this book will also encourage you as you continue to pursue God's purpose in making disciples of our young people—and not just fully devoted disciples, but fully developed disciples, disciples who not only act passionately and graciously but who also think deeply, wisely, and biblically.

Chapter Two
The Power of Paradigms

Paradigms are powerful. Indeed, our prevailing paradigms not only shape how we see the world but also shape our responses when the world as we know it begins to change. That we live in turbulent times does not surprise most of us. And although our world has changed dramatically during the past half century, I would suggest that our responses have not always been effective because many of the paradigms that have driven those responses have remained unchallenged and intact.

Constancy isn't always a bad thing. It can, however, create disaster when un-examined paradigms thwart our attempts to respond in an effective, timely fashion to the kinds of dramatic changes that we witnessed in the second half of the twentieth century and that accelerated dramatically in the first decade of the new millennium. So just what are paradigms, and why do they have such power to influence how we see and respond to the world around us?

Paradigms: A Definition

If you look up the word *paradigm* in a dictionary, you'll discover that the word is derived from the Greek word *paradeigma*, which simply means "model, pattern, example" (Barker 1993, 31). In the book *Paradigms*, Joel Barker provides us with a great definition that deepens our understanding of the concept and why it is important. He writes, "A paradigm is a set of rules and regulations (written or unwritten) that does two things: (1) it establishes or defines boundaries; and (2) it tells you how to behave inside the boundaries in order to be successful" (32).

Think about it for a minute. By using the definition above, you could understand your philosophy of education as a paradigm, so too your theology of education if you have one, and your current administrative and financial practice as well. Somewhere at some time—in a graduate school course, while reading a book, during a workshop presentation—someone captured your attention, and you adopted a paradigm. That paradigm may exist as "unquestioned, tacit understanding," but it does exist, and it does shape your thinking and practice regarding how best to organize and lead a Christian school.

Paradigms then have tremendous value because they provide us with a set of assumptions that allow us to think and act in a cohesive manner. They help us organize information in a predictable (therefore usable) way. They are not, however, to be viewed as absolute truth. Thus we must periodically reexamine our paradigms in the light of Scripture and wise practice. That is one of the goals of this book: to help you reexamine the paradigms that shape your thinking about how to fund a Christian school.

Current Prevailing Paradigms

Perhaps it would be helpful at this point to address some of the prevailing paradigms that I believe keep us from responding creatively to many of the problems currently plaguing Christian schools. I acknowledge that some will consider what I have to say highly subjective and that others will consider it a bit unfair. It is my hope, however, to spark a conversation, even a little tension. I believe a little creative conflict is healthful for any leadership team and essential to genuine problem-solving efforts.

Ministry Mentality

Here I'm not referring to a ministry heart. All of us should possess a ministry heart. We should care deeply about others while working diligently to fulfill God's call in our lives. Such words as *sacrifice, honor, grace, love,* and *passion* should describe us. Determining the true meaning of a ministry heart requires, however, careful thought and wise application. Here are a few illustrations that I hope will differentiate between a genuine ministry heart and the less-helpful ministry mentality.

That law of gravity thing, it doesn't apply to us

All of us—well, all of us who have a grip on reality—understand that we ignore certain physical laws at our peril. We may not be able to explain in formal, scientific detail all that is involved in, say, the law of gravity, but we do have a fairly good grasp on what happens to a human body when dropped from an airplane cruising at 10,000 feet. Fictional characters may leap tall buildings with a single bound. You and I, however, face restrictions because of certain scientific realities. We recognize those restrictions and act accordingly.

The law of perception, for example, may not rise to the same level as the law of gravity. But we ignore the law of perception at our peril, because as Mary Mitchell reminds us,

> First impressions often are as shallow as rain water on a leaky roof.
>
> Yet they are about as permanent as concrete, and if you're like most people, it would take at least a crowbar or an act of God to change them....
>
> [Perceptions] are important. They can make or break a budding relationship. And although we live in an age of technology, we cannot afford to forget that our relationships form the foundation of our work life.
>
> The fact is that receiving a first impression is an uncomplicated experience. On the other hand, giving a first impression, a positive first impression, can be anything but. (1998, xiii)

Most of you will nod knowingly in response to Mitchell's words. But do you really believe that what she is saying applies to you and to your school—I mean *really* believe? I encounter school leaders who may agree cognitively with that quotation but who behave as though they are somehow exempt or as though God will intervene in some miraculous manner to overturn the law of perception. They reason that God must—yes, *must*—honor His promises to bless people whose motives are pure and who are willing to work with diligence to fulfill a righteous purpose. In other words, they believe that hard work and good intentions will overcome lesser laws such as the law of perception. But real-world experiences prove that belief false.

9

Yes, God does at times intervene in remarkable ways, but most of the time we live with the consequences of our decisions and actions. If you make enough bad decisions, over time you dramatically increase the probability of failure. And contrary to much popular but flawed thinking, God is not obligated to ride in and rescue us from the consequences of sloppy thinking and poor execution. Remember this: the lesser laws apply to the children of God in the same way they apply to all beings created in the image of God. If you ignore that reality, you court disaster.

You may have an exceptional, highly motivated faculty. Your curriculum may be remarkable. Neither will matter, however, if perception doesn't match reality in the minds of potential customers.

Dimes into dollars

I've often remarked that Christian school administrators can turn a dime into a dollar better than almost anyone. I mean that as a compliment. Most administrators manage their budgets well. At times, however, saving money in the short term can have serious consequences.

Let's look at marketing as an illustration. You cannot find inexpensive ways to produce quality marketing materials and then launch a well-conceived, well-coordinated marketing strategy that will produce the desired results. In an age of special-effects-laden blockbusters, bargain-priced videos will seem amateurish. If you are not careful, you can unintentionally reinforce the powerful, prevailing perception that Christian school leaders, though well-meaning, are not very professional, capable people.

Another illustration is your purchase process. There is certainly nothing wrong with a good negotiation process. But never expect businesses to deliver for less than it costs them to operate. Believe me, you will benefit in the long run, both from a quality product and from the goodwill you generate, when you treat vendors in an honorable way.

Sadly, the ministry mentality drives the kind of thinking I've just described. The ministry mentality looks for the least expensive way to build and maintain buildings, to purchase equipment, to hire faculty and staff, and to do a hundred other things that are crucial to the quality of the program you want to offer. The ministry mentality leads you to believe that somehow you will find protection from the negative consequences of poor decisions and of false perceptions. The ministry mentality permits poor performance from faculty and staff because you value a good heart above excellent performance. In fact, the ministry mentality keeps you from understanding that excellence is not the enemy of virtue and compassion.

Professional Practices

Mark Eppler writes, "People have a tendency to fall in love with tools. Those 'tools' may be a favorite hammer, a preferred piece of software, or a long-established way of doing things. We return to them time and again, preferring their familiarity to the uncertainty of 'things different.' Our love affair with our tools often skews how we define a problem. Psychologist Abraham Maslow once said, 'If the only tool you have is a hammer, you treat everything like a nail' " (2004, 102).

I've often posed the following questions to administrators, teachers, and board members who attend my workshops: Why do we structure our middle schools and high schools the way we do? Why, for instance, do we break the day into six or seven class periods, each lasting fifty to sixty minutes? Why do we approach teaching individual disciplines the way we do? Why, for example, do we separate history from literature? Doesn't literature provide us with insight into the motivations of people of a particular time and place? If so, shouldn't we teach those subjects in tandem?

I find the answers to my questions most intriguing. Remember, I'm talking to education professionals—leaders and decision makers in our Christian schools. Here are the two most frequent answers: "I don't know" and "Well, that is the way we've always done it." Then I respond, "What body of research suggests that the way we currently structure our schools best helps students learn?" It is a trick question because no body of research, to my knowledge, indicates that the way we currently structure our schools makes sense from a teaching-learning perspective.

Clearly, however, we need some rather significant changes in the way we do school, especially given the enormous changes in technology currently reshaping our culture and economy. If not, we may be guilty of preparing students today for a world that existed yesterday.

The Most Powerful of Prevailing Paradigms

Perhaps nowhere have unexamined, prevailing paradigms shaped Christian schools more than in budgeting and finance. And perhaps no other paradigm has had a greater negative impact on the day-to-day operations of Christian schools.

Years ago a good friend of mine, Mickey Bowdon, and I sat down to dialogue about this problem. After several hours we created the bullet points listed below.

- The operational budget will be created with a gap.
- Teachers and staff will not be appropriately compensated.
- There will be insufficient resources allocated to program enhancement and facility maintenance.
- There will be an insufficient or nonexistent reserve fund.
- The gap will be covered through some form of fund-raising.
- The gap is necessary to keep tuition at affordable levels.

Carefully consider each point. Then ask yourself, "Does this accurately represent my approach to finance and budget development?" Be honest. At the time I am writing this, I have now presented the material in my finance enabler some thirty times to nearly 800 school administrators and board members. At every presentation I've asked the participants to challenge any point that doesn't accurately represent their own practice. As of this moment I've not heard anyone say, "We don't do it that way." I then follow my first question with a second, which I borrowed from Dr. Phil: "So how's that working for you?" The instantaneous response is now predictable. After a few brief, embarrassed chuckles, everyone says, "Not very well."

I then ask if anyone in the room can give me the definition of *insanity*. You know the answer: Insanity is present when a person continues to do the same thing the same way over and over again, hoping for a different outcome.

Using that definition, we can legitimately describe our current fiscal practices as insane. And although we all try to find ways to modify our approach by using different fund-raising strategies, the essential formula remains the same, as do the consequences. Perhaps it is time to reexamine the basic presuppositions of that formula.

I always ask a second question at that point in my presentation: "Is there another way?" The responses to that question are more hesitant, less assured. They are hoping the answer is yes, but they are not quite certain it is. At that point I try to assure them that we can indeed find another way, a better way, a way that more accurately reflects biblical principles and wise organizational practice. But I also acknowledge that the better way will require a different way of thinking, seeing, and then behaving. It will also require us to develop a communication strategy to change the way our school parents think so that they do not come unglued as we make necessary adjustments in our practice.

The primary goal of this book is to challenge and change the current Christian school funding paradigm. So let's begin that process by examining some key principles that cannot be ignored as we consider how best to rethink our paradigms and reorder our practices.

Chapter Three
The Nonnegotiables:
Biblical Principles

The Reality of the Box

We often hear that we can find the solution to almost any challenge only if we are willing to "get out of the box." But most of us live in very well-defined boxes from which we find it difficult if not impossible to extricate ourselves.

I don't disagree with the advice about boxes; I simply think we need to recognize that we always face elements in any situation that we can't change. Sometimes those elements lie beyond our control. For example, I once worked with a school whose enrollment had slowly declined over several years. The school's leaders contacted me in hopes that I could help them develop a more effective marketing strategy to reverse that decline.

I arrived on campus with my own personal paradigms firmly in place. I had no doubt I could help them, but after only a brief time with the school leadership team, I discounted most of the usual culprits that can create enrollment problems. As it turned out, two local companies that had provided substantial local employment had closed their doors several years before my visit. The closures devastated the local economy, forcing hundreds of families to relocate. The population of the town had dropped by more than 30 percent. Now take a guess at how much enrollment at the school had declined during those years. Good guess. The enrollment was down about 30 percent.

That kind of economic downturn and the resulting impact on local population are beyond the control of any school, anywhere. The school could take some fairly typical actions—develop better enrollment-management strategies and work to improve brand recognition, for example—but they had to live with certain realities beyond their control. In other words, they lived in a box, not on a blank canvas.

Most Christian school leaders simply cannot ignore the reality of the box, a fact that Mark Eppler reminds us isn't always a bad thing: "The box takes a beating in the creative process. Nothing of value, it would seem, ever occurs there. In reality, nothing of value can occur *without* the box. If creativity represents the flexible mind at work, the box represents the structure needed to give that creativity purposeful form.... [We must engage in problem solving approaches that provide] the mental flexibility to consider nonstandard options without discarding the benefits of structure (known truths)" (2004, 108).

Christian schools are not going to solve the difficult financial issues they face—issues that can and often do threaten a school's very existence—unless those schools break free from the wrong kinds of prevailing paradigms that prevent creativity. In addition, every school will face certain realities that create restraints in pursuit of financial health. In this chapter and in the two that follow, we will explore the kinds of nonnegotiables that a healthy organization needs. Once a school leadership team has identified those nonnegotiables and thereby has created the necessary structure for its box, then and only then can that team begin thinking and acting creatively within the realities it faces.

Biblical Principles: Our First Nonnegotiables

Are there any biblical principles that are so absolute, so clear, so compelling that they form the foundation you build your life on and shape how you pursue your vocation? I suspect there are. It is, therefore, my argument that there are indeed some universal biblical principles that must drive financial practice in Christian schools. I would further argue that we experience severe consequences whenever we ignore or purposely violate those biblical principles—those nonnegotiables that give our box structure as we deal creatively with reality.

In the introduction to his exceptional commentary on Proverbs, Derek Kidner gives us excellent insight into how biblical wisdom must shape our everyday decisions in not only our personal lives but our business lives as well:

> Proverbs ... offers a key to life ... a unifying approach to life, because it suits the most commonplace realms as fully as the most exalted. Wisdom leaves its signature on anything well made or well judged, from an apt remark to the universe itself, from a shrewd policy (which springs from practical insight) to a noble action (which presupposes moral and spiritual discernment). In other words, it is equally at home in the realms of nature and art, of ethics and politics, to mention no others, and forms a single basis of judgment for them all. (1964, 13)

What great insight! Kidner is explaining exactly what we do in our Christian schools. We take God's truth, explain that truth in terms our students can understand, and then we help them learn to think critically about how best to apply those truths in such a way that lives are transformed and God glorified. We need to do the same thing with every aspect of our schools, including how we manage and invest the financial resources provided to us by our Lord. Therefore I would ask you to consider the following.

Exploring Seven Key Biblical Principles

I have identified seven biblical principles for us to consider as we make financial decisions in our schools. You may not agree with all my thoughts. You may lengthen or shorten the list. But I don't want you to ignore the issue. I want you to engage. Challenge my assumptions and conclusions, but make your argument biblically sound and practically wise. We can no longer afford to avoid this discussion.

Principle 1: Calculate the Cost

"For which one of you, when he wants to build a tower, does not first sit down and calculate the cost to see if he has enough to complete it? Otherwise, when he has laid a foundation and is not able to finish, all who observe it begin to ridicule him, saying, 'This man began to build and was not able to finish' " (Luke 14:28–30, NASB).

God does sometimes ask us to journey into a world or a situation beyond our current understanding or experience. But when we exercise faith, we do not take some blind leap leading to an impetuous decision that typically results in a catastrophe from which we expect, even demand, that God rescue us. Instead, when we exercise faith, we choose to pursue the person and purposes of God with integrity, courage, and wisdom; and as God reminds us in the text from Luke, wisdom requires that we count the cost before pursuing our dreams and plans.

But time and time again, I converse with people who sincerely believe that God is somehow obligated to meet the needs of the school they lead simply because, in their words, "We are doing the right thing; we are doing God's will." Here is a truth to ponder. God never calls us to a task for which He does not equip us and for which He does not provide necessary resources. Yes, at times we must stretch beyond our current comfort zone. But God simply never asks us to act irresponsibly to accomplish His purposes.

You may be asking, "What does it mean in practical terms to count the cost?" Here are some thoughts:

- *Do your homework.* Thoroughly research the topic. If you are considering an expansion of facilities, then it makes sense to visit your local zoning and planning departments. You need to discover what you can and cannot do with your property. You need to develop a good sense for future development in your community. For example, you need to know about the plans for future housing developments, for additional retail infrastructure, and for any road projects. You always do well to develop relationships with people who work in those local departments.
- *Seek wise counsel.* Identify people of integrity who possess significant knowledge on the topic you are researching. Expand your search beyond people you know. Find the best, most respected person available. Ask questions, listen carefully, and invite the person's scrutiny. Equally important, learn whom not to involve in this discussion.
- *Determine actual and eventual costs.* Remember this: if the architect or the builder says the cost could be anywhere between $3 and $5 million, always count on the $5 million and then add at least 10 percent. Then do a study on how your new facility or new equipment or new program will increase your operating expenses. A new building will require additional

staff, preventive and ongoing maintenance, and utilities. You will eventually need to repair and replace equipment. Programs will also require new staff and new equipment. School leaders seldom do well when determining actual and eventual costs.

Principle 2: Determine the Worth

No school can ever achieve excellence without an exceptional staff. (Luke 10:7, 1 Timothy 5:17–18, and Proverbs 27:18 give us insight about this principle.) As Jim Collins observes, "The executives who ignited the transformations from good to great did not first figure out where to drive the bus and then get people to take it there. No, they *first* got the right people on the bus (and the wrong people off the bus) and *then* figured out where to drive it" (2001, 41).

Expanding that observation, I'd like to add a thought. Not only do we need the right people in the right seats on the bus, but we also need them to remain with us for the journey. Great people who become disillusioned leave, and often before they depart they infect others with a dreadful disease called disillusionment, which can wreak havoc in even the healthiest organization. The writer of Proverbs sends us this message: "Hope deferred makes the heart sick" (13:12, NIV). Even the most mature people grow frustrated over time when they have inadequate financial resources for even the simplest lifestyle.

Somehow over time the Church (and I use that term in the universal sense) has come to believe that it is acceptable, even saintly, to expect people in ministry to labor for a salary that by any estimation is far below the value the secular marketplace puts on the same kind of work. I can't use strong enough language in disagreeing with such a thoroughly unbiblical assumption.

Neither the Old nor the New Testament condones such an expectation. In ancient Israel God did not permit the Levites to own land. God set them apart to serve, and He did not want the obligation to engage in commerce to divert them. Not owning land, however, made them vulnerable because they had no means for creating private wealth. They depended fully on the support of the other tribes. That support was not voluntary. God designated a portion of the other tribes' tithe for the Levites' support.

The same obligation passed on to the early church. Paul addresses this issue in several ways. He reminds the members of the church at Corinth that it is completely appropriate for a pastor to receive compensation for his ministry (1 Corinthians 9:7–14, 2 Corinthians 11:7–9). In a letter to Timothy, Paul even gives an indication of the manner in which a pastor should receive compensation. Paul tells Timothy that a pastor who labors hard in the Word is worthy of double honor (1 Timothy 5:17). That passage has created some difficulties for various commentators. They want to find some other meaning to those words, but Paul is clearly saying that hard work in ministry should result in double the standard wage! Somehow we have managed to ignore those words.

In fact, we have built the Christian school movement largely on the backs of people who have worked for a fraction of what their colleagues in the public system make. It is long past time that we revisit our assumptions and change our practices. I am aware of the potential impact on the typical Christian school budget. My anecdotal research suggests that the average Christian school would at minimum need to double its budget if it chose to compensate its teachers on a level equal to that of the local public school. Few schools could easily manage that kind of adjustment to their budgets and the necessary impact on their tuition levels.

At this moment you are probably thinking, "Dr. Pue, don't you think we would increase teacher salaries if we could? We just can't. It isn't reasonable." I understand. I've sat at your desk. I spent fifteen years building budgets for a Christian school and five years with the same responsibility at a Christian college. I understand the challenges you face and the frustration you feel. I know you would do more if you believed you could. But we can't just throw our hands in the air and say, "There is nothing we can do about this problem." None of us are free to ignore either our Lord or market realities. If what Jesus says is true—and who would dispute that?—then a working person is truly worthy of his or her hire (Luke 10:7), and we have a responsibility to compensate that person appropriately. We have, it seems to me, an inescapable obligation.

Again I ask, "So how then should we respond?" Well, I think everyone would agree that it would be unwise to increase compensation to necessary levels all at once. It is time to become creative about finding ways to increase teacher salaries so that we can honestly say that we are compensating the workers in a manner worthy of the work we have asked them to do. I encourage you to consider these ideas as ways to address this difficult problem:

- Provide transitional and below-market housing. Many top-tier colleges and universities do that to attract exceptional faculty to areas of the country where even a modest house sells for $750,000. In some cases they have very sophisticated equity-sharing agreements that you might find a bit challenging, but you can choose other options. For example, approach investors who might be willing to purchase or even build apartments or condos. They could then lease those properties at below-market value. Over time the investors might even be willing to donate those properties to the school to take advantage of tax benefits.

- Reduce the size of your administrative staff and reallocate those resources to increase teacher salaries. I am convinced that most schools are overstaffed. Most schools operate in a highly inefficient manner. Overstaffing may not be occurring at your school, but I encourage you to invite someone to your school to do a staff audit. I think you may find the results surprising.

- Outsource as many functions as you can. You are not, for example, in the tuition collection business, and you probably do it poorly. Outsource. You are not in the cleaning business, so outsource. Consider outsourcing anything not absolutely essential to your core business.

- Create endowments specifically targeted at funding the compensation of lead teachers or department heads. Colleges have been doing so for centuries. They recognize the importance of attracting and retaining the best for key teaching positions.

- Help your teachers find worthwhile summer employment. The primary wage earners almost always need to find a way to supplement their income during the summer. Some of your teachers possess gifts and skills that make them very attractive to local businesses. Some of them have the ability to start their own businesses. Find a way to increase the amount you assist these teachers in finding summer employment.

Principle 3: Understand the Obligation

Paul gives us this insight about principle 3: "But if anyone does not provide for his own, and especially for those of his household, he has denied the faith and is worse than an unbeliever" (1 Timothy 5:8, NASB). I've never talked to a Christian school administrator who hasn't experienced the loss of an exceptional teacher who simply could not provide for his or her family. And the problem is increasing. Housing prices often make it impossible for teachers in Christian schools to own a home.

And what about health care? The trajectory of insurance rates resembles that of a Saturn rocket launching the space shuttle into orbit. Purchased an automobile recently? Have you recovered from the sticker shock? What is your response to your monthly utility bills? Living even a simple life in America today is remarkably expensive, often beyond the reach of a head of household who is teaching in a Christian school.

If we cannot or will not compensate our teachers in a reasonable manner, we are simply going to find ourselves unable to attract and retain quality people. Those people have an obligation to their families that supersedes their obligation to our schools. God takes that responsibility seriously; that is why Paul uses such strong language in his letter to Timothy.

Once again I can hear the objections. "Dr. Pue, if people are called to a ministry of teaching, then they have no choice but to respond to that call in obedience. They must have faith that God will meet their needs." I think we've already had this conversation, but let me respond to those statements. The question still remains: "How does God typically provide for our needs? Few of us walked outside today to discover our lawn littered with manna. God did not intend His gift of manna to Israel to be a normative occurrence. As soon as the Israelites arrived in the Land of Promise, God expected them to work hard and exercise wise stewardship in a land flowing with milk and honey. We earn our bread through the sweat of our brow.

Are there times when God chooses to meet our needs in an unusual, even miraculous manner? Of course. I can offer several remarkable stories as illustrations of that reality. We, however, step into dangerous territory when we seek to elevate what the Scriptures clearly present as unusual to the norm. God used ravens to feed a prophet (1 Kings 17:2–6), and God miraculously replaced a widow's store of flour and oil (1 Kings 17:12–16). Those are great events, encouraging events. They remind us of God's enduring love and provision. God did not reveal them to us, however, as model economic plans. If you are depending on birds to bring you your food, I suspect that you are going to become very hungry.

God expects us to provide for our families, and we do that primarily through our labor. We must stop making people feel guilty about leaving the teaching ministry if they leave because they don't make enough money to provide the essentials of life. If we want to keep quality teachers, we must simply accept the obligation to pay the worker what he or she is worth.

Principle 4: Keep Your Promises

If "hope deferred makes the heart sick" (Proverbs 13:12, NIV), then promises broken devastate the soul. If you paused for just a moment to scroll through the database of your life, how long do you think it would take before your memory captured a time when someone you trusted violated that trust? A minute? A fraction of a minute? For some reason our minds seldom forget that kind of event.

Why do you think memory works that way? Could it be that we expect more from those in whom we have placed our trust? Could it be that many of those people have encouraged us to trust them? Could it be that our first impulse as a child of God is to trust those in positions of holy leadership? Could it be that we intuitively understand that without trust an organization cannot achieve its goals? Could it be all those reasons and more?

In the book *The Five Dysfunctions of a Team*, Patrick Lencioni writes, "Trust lies at the heart of a functioning, cohesive team. Without it, teamwork is all but impossible" (2002, 195). I couldn't agree more. Remember the earlier principle I noted. You cannot violate God's principles in pursuit of God's purposes and expect God to bless you. Nothing does more violence to God's design than a lack of integrity.

There are times, however, when circumstances beyond our control force us to make difficult financial decisions. So what do you do when a genuine, unexpected financial crisis hits and you can survive in the short term only by reducing expenses, a situation that typically means reducing the cost of staffing? Let me offer some thoughts:

- Don't give in to the temptation to make cuts that affect your ability to deliver what you've promised to your students and parents. Nothing screams "sinking ship" faster than cutting a vital program. It changes in a negative way the value equation we'll talk about in detail later. It also reduces trust, a situation that has a way of reducing your enrollment. Then you are caught in a downward spiral that you will find difficult to reverse.

- Go to your core donors and seek their help in bridging the crisis. You have the opportunity to do so once every ten years. Chronic crises will quickly dry up your sources of gift revenue. Explain with complete honesty what has occurred. Present your short- and long-term plans to respond to the current situation. Prepare to explain why your plans make sense now and in the future. Promise to keep your donors informed about your progress. Follow through on that promise.

- If you don't have enough core donors, go to your local bank and seek a bridge loan. Everything I said in the preceding point applies here.

- It may be time to reevaluate your staffing situation. Don't cut staff members who affect vital services. You may find, however, those inefficiencies I mentioned earlier. You may need to eliminate a position. If you do, make sure you provide adequate notice.

- I would rather see an organization cut positions than consider across-the-board reductions in salaries or benefits. Nothing creates resentment faster than taking away something already given.

- If you have no other option, you must ensure that any sacrifice is shared sacrifice. That sharing includes every member of the board. No board should ever ask a staff to accept a reduction in salary without accepting the same reduction itself. How, you may ask, can the board share in a salary reduction? It is this simple. If the board asks the staff to take a 10 percent cut in pay, the board members should each take a similar cut by increasing their giving to the school by the equivalent of 10 percent of their current salary. That's not going to happen, you say. Here is my response. If your board members will not share the sacrifice, they have no business asking the staff to accept a reduction in pay. Find another solution. Keep your promises.

I don't think we understand how seriously God takes this principle. Listen to what Solomon has to say on this topic: "When you make a vow to God, do not delay in fulfilling it. He has no pleasure in fools; fulfill your vow. It is better not to vow than to make a vow and not fulfill it. Do not let your mouth lead you into sin. And do not protest to the temple messenger, 'My vow was a mistake.' Why should God be angry at what you say and destroy the work of your hands?" (Ecclesiastes 5:4–6, NIV). Now what do you think? Keep your promises.

Principle 5: Instruct the Wealthy

If you need a purpose statement for your development program, let me suggest these words from the apostle Paul: "Instruct those who are rich in this present world ... to do good, to be rich in good works, to be generous and ready to share" (1 Timothy 6:17–19, NASB). Paul clearly understands the power and allure of money, as well as its capacity for good and for evil. At no time and in no place, however, does Paul put wealth creation in a negative light.

Understand that the number one reason why people don't give to your school is simply that you have never asked them to give. The number two reason is that they have not been well taught about biblical stewardship. The number three reason is that they don't share your passion. The number four reason is that they don't have confidence in your ability to deliver your mission with excellence. And a fifth reason exists for parents: they see their relationship with the school as a simple exchange of value. They reason thus: I pay you tuition in return for an education; that tuition should be enough to provide the education I seek for my child.

Most people will not subsidize the education of someone else's child. Most people don't understand how you fund capital expenses. Most people don't want to hear that the cost of tuition is increasing. Most people don't understand the design of your budget. They want a Lexus education for the price of a Chevy Cobalt education. That misguided expectation is reality. Your job is to change that reality.

As a school leader, you can do nothing more important. Others can develop better instructional strategies or work to improve the curriculum or coach the girls' volleyball team to a state championship. You must take on the goal of building strategic partnerships with key people who have the financial capacity to make a significant difference in the ability of your school to deliver its mission with excellence. You must not only help those who have the gift of giving to better understand their stewardship obligations, but also demonstrate the wisdom of investing in the lives of your students and faculty.

Principle 6: Represent with Accuracy

In the eighth chapter of Paul's letter to the Romans, we find this compelling and comforting statement: "And we know that God causes all things to work together for good to those who love God, to those who are called according to His purpose" (v. 28, NASB). To discover God's purpose for us, we must move on to the next verse, where Paul continues his thought: "For those whom He foreknew, He also predestined to become conformed to the image of His Son." God's goal, God's purpose for our lives, is to help us conform to the image of God's Son and then to live that life in full view of a watching world.

In fact, God gives the world permission to determine the authenticity of our claims to be God's children by how we behave in public. Do we love our brothers and sisters in practical, visible ways? If not, the world has the right to conclude that we are not the children of God. Do we live in unity and peace with our brothers and sisters? If not, the world has the right to conclude that we are delivering a false message. If God gives unbelievers the right to judge the validity of our faith by how closely we mirror the Creator, then how much more important is it that we accurately represent our Creator to the children we serve?

Think how often in chapel or in a Bible class or just in the course of conversation we tell our students how awesome God is. He is, we declare, the great Creator God, who by the power of His spoken word brought the world into existence. And what a world it is! We don't live in a one-dimensional, gray-toned world but in a world of remarkable beauty, fascinating diversity, and endless opportunity—all because the God in whose image we are made and whose image we are supposed to represent is a God of beauty, creativity, and purpose.

Now take a walk around your buildings and through your classrooms. Honestly evaluate the quality of your faculty, staff, and resources. Then ask yourself this question: Do we as a school and do I as a leader accurately represent God to the children we teach and the community we seek to influence?

Why is this accurate representation so important? I suspect you already have an answer to that question. It is important because our students and our community come to understand the nature of God not just by the words we speak but also by all we do. If we speak one truth but act in opposition to it, we send conflicting, confusing messages that lead people to incorrect conclusions about the God we worship and serve.

Principle 7: Recognize Your Responsibility to the Poor

I didn't grow up poor, but like many Americans my family lived one paycheck away from disaster. And when my mom and dad separated and then divorced while I was in junior high school, the situation became even more precarious. I never missed a meal, though a lot of them consisted of ten-for-a-dollar potpies and creamed chipped beef on toast (a true culinary delight). But when our church started a Christian school, we simply could not afford the fifty-dollar-a-month tuition.

I could attend Dade Christian School only because the leaders of the church I attended created a job for me. I became a maintenance engineer, a janitor if you will, and the church paid me the princely sum of one dollar an hour. It wasn't much, but it was enough to cover my tuition each month. I will forever be grateful for the opportunity I received.

Because the cost of education is escalating at a frightening pace, the number of families who find it increasingly difficult if not impossible to pay the tuition you charge is growing. This situation presents us with a difficult challenge. If, as I will argue later, we must charge what it costs us to provide a quality education, how can we ensure that all families who truly want a Christian education for their children can have access to that education? That is a fair question.

I think we must first, however, decide whether we should make education accessible. Notice I didn't say affordable. Education simply isn't affordable. It is expensive, and it is growing increasingly so. *Affordable* is the wrong paradigm from which to develop our budgeting process. Making education *accessible* to people who have a genuine need and a genuine desire for Christian schooling is, however, a noble and biblical goal. Consider the following texts from Proverbs:

- "Do not withhold good from those to whom it is due, when it is in your power to do it. Do not say to your neighbor, 'Go, and come back, and tomorrow I will give it,' when you have it with you" (3:27–28, NASB).
- "There is one who scatters, and yet increases all the more, and there is one who withholds what is justly due, and yet it results only in want. The generous man will be prosperous, and he who waters will himself be watered" (11:24–25).
- "One who is gracious to a poor man lends to the Lord, and He will repay him for his good deed" (19:17).
- "He who is generous will be blessed, for he gives some of his food to the poor" (22:9).

These are compelling words. How people use their wealth tells us more about the character of those people than probably anything else. Christian school leaders face a difficult reality. Compassion always comes with a price tag. Education is expensive. Someone must pay. So how do we make education accessible? I will address the answer to that question in some detail later in this book, but let me introduce a thought at this point.

We do not lack the resources to provide financial aid, even substantial financial aid. However, we, and here I mean the Christian school movement as a whole, have failed to make our case to the right people in a compelling way. People give enormous sums of money each year to international missions projects, but people give comparatively little to Christian schooling at all levels. The latter must change. Many in the Christian school movement fear that the time will come when only the wealthy will be able to access a Christian school education. Unless schools take purposeful, strategic action to build a strong, sustainable financial foundation apart from tuition revenue, we will probably experience that fear as a reality.

Conclusion

I know that you have found this chapter difficult to read and ponder. It certainly has not been my goal to increase your sense of frustration, but I'm convinced that we can no longer ignore either reality or biblical mandate. Be encouraged, however, because solutions exist for the issues I've raised.

We've identified one portion of our planning box. But we have not finished. Biblical principles are nonnegotiable. Now we need to continue building by using personal and philosophical preference to explore your school's specific nonnegotiable characteristics. This process will require great wisdom, reflection, and honesty.

Chapter Four
Finding Your Core: Another Kind of Nonnegotiable

Years ago few, if any, ministry organizations developed a mission statement. But today, driven by accreditation requirements or the relentless pressure of business and ministry gurus, school boards and ministry leaders all across the country have labored to craft a statement they say describes the essence of their church, school, or organization—and always in twenty-five words or fewer, of course!

The backlash to this change has been predictable. Some people view creating mission statements as another useless activity that produces nothing more substantial than empty pizza boxes and a document that staff, board, and constituents take no more seriously than they do monthly newsletters and weekly progress reports.

We can understand such skepticism. I have rarely seen a situation in which a leadership team can point to specific decisions that its organization's mission statement clearly shaped. Indeed, I find few organizations in which staff or constituents can even quote the mission statement with a reasonable level of accuracy. Like most strategic-planning documents, most mission statements make remarkably little impact on the day-to-day life of organizations.

So was all that effort and energy wasted? No! Every ministry needs to discover and define its primary purpose if it is going to make wise decisions about how best to use its resources or whom to make part of its team. In fact, I believe that next to the people an organization hires, nothing is as important to it as the purpose it chooses to pursue.

Indeed, if a ministry is going to stay true to its core beliefs and calling, it must periodically step aside from the routine in order to review and confirm its core, to remember its calling. Failure to do so inevitably results in the kind of drift that severs organizations from their roots. Leaders and constituents must keep first things first in their minds, and that focus doesn't take place accidentally. It requires frequent, intentional effort.

First, I think you must literally keep the mission visible. A person visiting your facility or reading any material about your school should encounter your mission and other characteristics of your core. Every communication with your parents and various publics should in some way remind them of what is important at your school.

Second, your core needs to serve as the compass by which you drive the direction of your school. This question should guide every decision by your administration and board: How will this action advance or reflect our school's core? Too often the question we ask is, How will this help us better market our school? That is not a bad question. It just isn't the right first question.

Third, every new staff person, every new faculty member, and every new board member should go through a thorough orientation process that communicates the school's core. No one should sense any ambiguity about what is essential.

Fourth, you should periodically go aside for substantial periods of review and reflection regarding your core. I strongly believe in well-designed retreats. You can think reflectively only if you step aside from your daily routine. It is difficult to think reflectively in the middle of your daily responsibilities, and if you don't practice reflective thinking you will think and behave reactively, and that kind of leadership always leads to negative consequences. Always. If Jesus found it necessary to go aside periodically, why do we believe it is unnecessary for us to do the same? When you don't take the time to ask "What if?" and "Why?" you will find yourself asking "What was that, and where did it come from?"

The Core: Defining the Truly Important

So just what is this core I keep talking about? The core is what you consider nonnegotiable about your school, church, or organization. Beyond adhering to the biblical principles we have explored, you must identify all those characteristics about which you will not compromise. You may create a short or long list of items that make up your particular core, but you must create a clear and understandable core, and those who deliver and live that core must fully own it.

For me the core consists of the following components: *beliefs, purpose, mission, values,* and *desired outcomes* or impact. To help in discovering your core, it is helpful to answer the following five questions.

Question 1: Why Do We Exist?

Purpose answers the why question: Why do we exist? It is the most important of all the questions we must ask ourselves. Without a clear answer you have no sustainable foundation upon which to build the enterprise that is your school. Without answering this question you cannot develop an instructional strategy, you cannot effectively market your school, you cannot wisely choose your faculty and staff, you cannot fairly evaluate your impact, and you cannot build the strategic partnerships you will so desperately need to fund your mission. Without a fully understood purpose, you are set on a journey for which you have no clear destination or means to ensure that you have ever arrived. Thus you are likely doomed to wander about in the wilderness, much like the nation of Israel.

In this brief space it is simply impossible to adequately address this crucial task. I can only plead with you to truly and fully answer the question, Why do we exist?

Question 2: What Must We Do to Fulfill Our Purpose?

Whereas *purpose* answers the why question, *mission* responds to the what questions: What must we do to fulfill our purpose? What primary activities must we engage in if we are going to effectively accomplish our purpose?

Let me illustrate what I mean. The purpose of the church is to make disciples. The mission of the church, the what-to-do-now, consists of the following: preaching, baptizing, teaching, praying, building community, serving one another, and worshipping. Those are the means we employ in making disciples. If you study the book of Acts carefully and then look at Paul's letters to the churches and to Timothy and Titus, you will see that Luke and Paul address those components again and again.

By the way, you will find the how-tos—the particular methodologies—uniformly missing in the Scriptures. When it comes to function, the Scriptures are clear; as to form, however, the Scriptures allow for great freedom. Thus when we as school leaders start the mission conversation, we should not begin by discussing instructional strategies or curricular theories. Rather, we should start by discussing the key elements of an educational experience and how those elements will facilitate our attempts to make disciples.

If we are honest, we must admit that much of what we do in our schools we have simply adopted, perhaps with some modifications, from current and historical educational practice. Seldom do school leaders take the time to question whether the approaches they employ accomplish the core purpose they have identified. We need to be more curious about the cause-and-effect relationship between methodology and outcome. A serious discussion of mission will force you to provide clarity about why you do what you do. It will also force you to practice both care in your choices and consistency in your practice, and when done well it will have enormous impact on your annual and strategic budgeting decisions.

Question 3: What Values and Commitments Will Shape Our Actions?

Next I recommend you ask yourself this question: How will we behave, or what will characterize us, as we seek to pursue our mission and fulfill our purpose? The answers you give to this question will do more than anything to determine the ethos, the environment, of your school.

Our *values* typically arise from what we believe. For instance, if you believe that students learn best in a highly structured environment, then your school will probably reflect that belief. During my tenure as head of school, I came to value creativity. I discovered by observation and research that creative teachers make the greatest impact on their students.

Thus creativity as a value began to make an impact on key actions, from hiring decisions to curriculum choices to teaching methodologies to room organization to teacher evaluation. I discovered, for example, that creative teachers respond negatively to rigid curricular designs. They want the freedom to modify teaching methodologies in pursuit of agreed-upon outcomes. In a creative approach to teaching, outcomes trump inputs every time. Unless a school values creativity properly defined, that school will probably not journey down the road I've just described.

What do you value? Who shares those values? Do those values shape decisions? Do they mark your school? Are they nonnegotiable? Are you willing to staff on the basis of those values, budget on the basis of those values, recruit students on the basis of those values, build a curricular and cocurricular program on the basis of those values, market your school on the basis of those values, live or die on the basis of those values? On any point at which you are willing to compromise, you have identified a nonvalue.

Question 4: What Do We Hope to Accomplish in the Lives of Our Students? What Is Our Desired Impact?

In the Christian school movement at large, I find a reluctance to put ourselves on record regarding meaningful *outcomes*. Oh, we are proud of how our students perform on standardized tests. I'm not talking about those kinds of outcomes. I am referring to the kinds of life outcomes that should set Christian schools apart.

We tell people, for example, that we are going to teach their children a biblical worldview. In reality, we have more trouble than we want to admit even defining a biblical worldview, much less providing research data demonstrating that our students actually live out a biblical worldview during their college years and beyond. I even wonder what would happen if we tested worldview understanding among those who serve on our faculties, staffs, and governing boards!

So what outcomes have you identified—outcomes that drive your decision-making process, that inform your budgeting decisions, and that energize your marketing and resource-development activities? What impact are you making that is so public and so powerful that it is attracting the attention of parents, pastors, and potential donors?

Remember, I'm not talking about inputs. I'm not talking about what you are going to teach or how you are going to teach it. I'm not talking about facilities, faculty, programs, or equipment. I'm talking about desired outcomes. I'm talking about impact. I'm talking about the evidence that all the inputs you talk about really make a difference in the lives of the students entrusted to your care.

If, for example, the ability to think critically is an outcome you desire, what evidence will you seek that might demonstrate that your students and graduates can indeed think critically? Do you desire to see continuous spiritual formation in the lives of your students? What about selfless service to the community and in the local church? What about the ability to engage secular culture with wisdom and confidence? Are your students and graduates "in love" with the Savior—passionate about deepening their relationship with Him? And how would you know any of that?

I don't know what outcomes you desire, but I know this. You must identify those outcomes. You must design curricular and cocurricular strategies you believe can produce those outcomes. You must then gather information that helps confirm or challenge your assumptions and strategies. I can't express how vital this process is. You will never generate the enrollment and support you need until you can carry out this process well. Your ability or lack thereof has significant budgeting implications.

Question 5: What Are Our Foundational Theological and Philosophical Beliefs?

Even though I placed *beliefs* first on my list and see the topic as foundational to all I have already said, I have waited until last to address what I mean by beliefs. I've done so because we face more difficulty nailing down our beliefs than we do all the other elements of our box. I think this is true for three key reasons.

First of all, beliefs in the contemporary Christian school movement vary significantly. Members of our fraternity espouse dozens of ideas, many of which are competing and even contradictory. Our schools represent the vast differences of opinion that exist in the evangelical church.

Second, in spite of all our discussions on worldview, theology, educational philosophy, management theory, and instructional strategy, we remain remarkably fuzzy on what we really believe, why we believe it, and the implications of that belief. I speak at many Christian school conferences during the course of a year. The variety of workshops offered always surprises me. The various assumptions, assertions, and presuppositions on which many of those workshops are based fascinate me even more. I'm not suggesting that variety is bad, but it does reveal a remarkably fluid understanding of what any given school might understand to be Christian schooling.

Third, I must confess my growing discomfort at the increasing influence of postmodern thought in our schools. Here I want to express caution because I sometimes find myself agreeing with some of what the more thoughtful postmodernists say. I do agree, for example, that we must be aware of how much our culture, history, and experience shape how we view events and interpret texts. Having said that, I would reiterate what Richard Weaver observed in the book *Ideas Have Consequences*: "This is society, in which the human being has a sense of direction; literally, it might be said, he knows 'up' from 'down,' because he knows where the higher goods are to be looked for. It is possible for him to live on the plane of spirit and intelligence *because some points of reference are fixed*" (1948, 36; italics added).

Written more than sixty years ago, Weaver's marvelous book powerfully reminds us of the catastrophic consequences awaiting a culture that abandons the idea of objective, knowable truth that applies to all people in all places at all times. Ideas do indeed have consequences. What you believe or do not believe matters. And when you make difficult decisions, you should not easily abandon your beliefs.

Ideas do have consequences. You must, therefore, identify those ideas and beliefs that you and your school consider nonnegotiable. You must then hire people who share those ideas, build policies and programs consistent with those ideas, and relentlessly remind your constituents and community why those ideas are important to you as you pursue your purpose, fulfill your mission, and live out your values.

Conclusion

If you fail to define your school in a manner consistent with the ideas I've introduced in this chapter, you will experience difficulty maintaining your integrity, crafting consistent policies, and making difficult choices about limited resources. Your school will probably suffer from mission drift, wasted resources, and staff problems. Community impact will decrease, and support will dwindle. Students will feel confused, and they will become more vulnerable as they transition into the more hostile climate they almost always find in higher education.

It is tempting to ignore this exercise. You may seek to cast a wide net to increase the pool of potential students. You fear that precision in defining yourself will cost you students. Your fears are justified. When you make clear who you are, some people will remove you from their choice set. So what? In my experience those are the people who cause much of your frustration. A prophet wisely asked, "Can two walk together, except they be agreed?" (Amos 3:3, KJV).

But remember, the idea here is to identify your nonnegotiables. Elevating personal preference to the level of essential element will have a debilitating effect on any school or organization. I believe that the list of what is nonnegotiable is not lengthy. You may want to read *The Five Most Important Questions You Will Ever Ask About Your Organization* by Peter Drucker (2008). I also strongly suggest that schools use the assistance of a trained facilitator who not only can guide the process but also can provide the level of objectivity crucial to the success of this process.

As a leader you must own the task of ensuring that the school you lead "stays the course." To do that well, you must decide what is truly important, develop strategies to implement the programs that will best advance what is truly important, and then build budgets that support your efforts.

Chapter Five
A Final Nonnegotiable: What's Excellence Got to Do with It?

People crave excellence, and in our culture they have come to expect excellence. Dozens of books—from *In Search of Excellence* (Peters and Waterman 1982) to *Good to Great* (Collins 2001) to *What Clients Love* (Beckwith 2003)—remind us of this reality. Indeed, an expectation of excellence has such a powerful grip on how Americans think that it has a major influence on how people in our country make all kinds of decisions, including decisions about the education of their children and about their giving. You simply can't ignore this reality and survive.

This reality makes some people a bit uncomfortable. And I understand why many in Christian school education feel uncomfortable in a conversation about excellence. Most Christian school leaders are purpose driven. They do not consider school leadership just a career; they consider it a calling, a holy vocation. And staff and faculty typically view their work the same way. Most, just like you, have accepted their call and pursued their passion because they strongly believe that Christian schooling is not simply another educational option but a crucial component of true biblical discipleship.

Thus staff and faculty feel significant pain, as you do, when dealing with parents who don't share that passion. Most Americans' understanding of the purpose of education remains firmly anchored in the cultural ideal and in their own idealized experiences as students themselves. Most are naive. Educational bling seduces and blinds them: the well-furnished science labs, the rows of computers, the extensive library, the athletic and fine arts facilities, and the promise of a Division I scholarship for their talented son or daughter. Worldview? Theology? Strong role models? Encouraging peers? Most parents believe they can find those at church.

I share your frustration, but it's time to get over it. What I just described and what you experience daily is reality. We live in that world, so you must compete in that world. We need to explore, however, a second—even more important—component in this conversation on excellence.

It Was Good

In Genesis 1 we read the following repeated refrain in the creation account: "And God saw that it was good." The refrain captures a fundamental reality about the nature of God as revealed in His creative activities. All He does, He does with excellence. Even in its fallen condition, the world we inhabit possesses such beauty that we often stare at a beautiful sunset or a majestic vista, stunned and silent as we marvel at the revelation of His imagination in His creation.

In our role as image bearers, God calls us to "be conformed" to that image as fully and accurately as we can (Romans 8:29, NKJV). Since excellence is such a critical part of that image, we simply cannot ignore the obligation to do all, even the most humble activity, with visible excellence. Thus we need to see excellence as an overall nonnegotiable; it must describe how we adhere to the biblical nonnegotiables and how we live out our core.

But what does excellence look like? How can we know that we have done something with excellence? Isn't excellence, like beauty, simply a cultural construct or a totally subjective determination? Can we really use some objective standard by which we can observe something and say, "That was done with excellence"? I believe we can, and I believe we can find the key to understanding excellence in the simple statement "And God saw that it was good."

If as image bearers we possess the capacity to create with excellence, doesn't it make sense that we also possess the ability to observe or taste or listen or read or engage and then decide, "That was good"? Sure, all our evaluations reflect some element of subjectivity. What is good clam chowder to me may not be good to you. But even though we may not always agree that a particular clam chowder is the best chowder or that a particular style of music is best, I suspect we can all agree that most people are right most of the time when discerning the mediocre from the amazing.

Think of it this way. Every parent who visits your school or enrolls his or her children in your school or even hears about your school from a friend or an acquaintance is making judgments—judgments about your facilities, the appearance of your buildings, the size and appearance of your classrooms, the cleanliness of your hallways and restrooms, the number of windows, the lighting, the repair or disrepair of doorways, your landscaping or lack of landscaping. Do people see attractive, inviting, and professional offices and classrooms, or do they see cluttered, chaotic, and confusing ones? Do they see torn and stained carpet? Do they see clean and polished floors? Do they see well-appointed labs? Does the furniture match? People will encounter an almost endless number of things visual that will shape their conclusions about you.

And while different people will certainly bring different expectations about different aspects of your school, they will all share a desire for excellence. And they will walk away from every encounter with your school having decided, "That was good," or having decided, "Not so much."

So Where Do You Go from Here?

At this point you may be tempted to respond, "Everyone would love to do things with excellence. Few Christian schools, however, possess the resources necessary to achieve excellence. We will never have facilities as well-appointed as those of the local public school. Our athletic and fine arts programs will always lag behind, as will our ability to keep up with the latest technology. We do the best we can with what we have. People just have to understand our reality."

But people don't. They may sympathize with you. They may even encourage you. In the end, however, people will most often choose what they believe to be best for their children. If they don't believe that you can deliver educational excellence, they will seek other options.

Money alone can't buy excellence because excellence is first and foremost a state of mind that insistently pushes us beyond our current performance and that refuses to accept the status quo.

I love this observation by Joel Barker in describing the concept of Total Quality Management. He writes, "Part of Total Quality Management is continuous improvement, or *kaizen* as the Japanese call it. *Kaizen* is all about the ability to make very small improvements in processes and products every day. Every day you are expected to find some way to get just one-tenth of 1 percent improvement in what you do or make" (1993, 80).

He continues by describing how we Americans tend to view progress and why we need to rethink our approach. "In the old American paradigm of management and product development, this seemed like a waste of time. Americans wanted to hit home runs. Big changes were all that were valued. And yet when you take one tenth of 1 percent daily improvement over a 240-day work year, you find that you have improved by 24 percent" (Barker 1993, 80). The apostle Paul refers to this facet of excellence when he prays that the church in Thessalonica will continue to "excel still more" (1 Thessalonians 4:1, NASB) and when he reminds those of the church in Philippi that we have not yet obtained perfection so we must continue to "press on" (Philippians 3:12–14).

If Barker is right, excellence does not result from trying to implement a major strategic initiative so much as it does from deciding to do even the smallest activity in a remarkable way. If your facility looks a bit worn, you could wait until someone decides to give you the money to renovate, or you could ask yourself, "What's the first thing we can do to begin the transformation today and continue it tomorrow?" Begin small rather than wait for the miraculous.

The Most Good for the Least Amount

Let me illustrate the concept of the most good for the least amount. In 1984, as head of Pike Creek Christian School, I faced a huge challenge: how to rebuild a badly tarnished brand. If building a brand is tough, rebuilding one is remarkably more difficult. Telling people that things have changed does not suffice; they need to see the changes. People must see visible, unmistakable changes in order to believe that those changes represent a serious, long-term commitment to excellence. Those kinds of changes cost money. We didn't have any. So what could we do?

It was then that I discovered *In Search of Excellence* by Thomas J. Peters and Robert H. Waterman (1982). It opened my eyes to a new way of thinking and led me to consider two key issues: customer service and innovation.

I decided to first address customer service because poor customer service characterizes most organizations and because it contributes significantly to retention problems. In the case of a school, we need to focus on two categories of customers: parents and students. Even though we must be purpose driven and not market driven in our mission, we need to understand that market forces must drive how we serve our customers. For us that understanding meant we had to find better ways than parent-teacher conferences and newsletters to communicate with our customers. Thus we made it our first priority to find ways to improve face-to-face communication with parents and students. And what did that improvement cost us? Virtually nothing. Big impact for little financial investment.

We set a second goal of finding ways to lead the discussion on educational innovation rather than always arriving as late responders. Guess what we discovered? Innovation is not expensive. It does require a willingness to do some research. It does require a willingness to consider nontraditional options. It does require a bit of creativity. And yes, on occasion it does require a bit of capital. If you have a history of innovation and a reasonably sound annual-fund program, however, you will find it much easier to raise funds for specific projects. Money follows innovation. When people see your commitment, they are more likely to fund your projects. Again, big impact for little financial investment.

We took the next step in our rebranding strategy by creating a visual perception that Pike Creek Christian School was a school of excellence. We created a completely new print image consisting of a new logo, new stationery, and new enrollment materials. We incurred a minimal cost because we hired a graphic arts student rather than a major firm to create the design.

We then pursued our next goal of dramatically improving the curb appeal of our buildings through a landscaping project and new signage. We achieved this goal largely through the sweat equity of our parents and of our sponsoring-church members. Next came painting projects, both interior and exterior, followed by some interior decor efforts that continued to build the perception that Pike Creek Christian School was a school of excellence. In ten years, our enrollment increased by over 250 percent.

Please understand that none of this growth would have been possible without the consistent, excellent performance of our faculty and staff. Excellence is not just perception; it is also reality. Either you are achieving excellence, or you are not. Either you have committed to excellence, or you have not. And your customers won't take long to discover the truth. When we committed to excellence, we didn't simply commit to a rebranding strategy. When people commit to excellence, they are committing to something much deeper, more profound. People and schools can achieve excellence only if they refuse to accept the status quo seemingly imposed by external forces, only if they truly believe they can be better tomorrow at what they do than they are today, and only if they relentlessly pursue a better future for their school and for their students.

Eight Key Commitments

I've talked a bit about why excellence is important and a bit about how to begin taking small, measured steps toward excellence. Now I'd like to take us down a slightly different path. I want to look at eight commitments a school must make to achieve excellence. When people—whether parents, students, supporters, or pastors—observe these elements at work in a school, they are more likely to see the school as excellent.

In the end a great facility and quality marketing materials can give you only this: the opportunity to make your case. That opportunity is certainly crucial, but alone it isn't enough. To those foundational elements you must add visible excellence, excellence that drives and defines everything you do and everyone who belongs to your team. If people can't see excellence regularly, they will probably conclude that your school rarely achieves excellence. In that case they will find it easier to walk away. No school can keep everyone in the fold. But if a school has quality people who daily demonstrate a commitment both to Christ and to an exceptional educational experience, that school will experience not only higher recruitment numbers but higher retention numbers as well.

1. Sacrifice

Sacrifice characterized the life of Christ, who reminds us, "Whoever wishes to be first among you shall be your slave; just as the Son of Man did not come to be served, but to serve" (Matthew 20:27–28, NASB). I suspect many of you are thinking, "But sacrifice is what we do every day as teachers and school leaders. Just teaching for the salary we receive is a sacrifice. People should know, understand, and honor that." Perhaps, but the kind of sacrifice I'm talking about goes deeper. It means tutoring a struggling student that extra hour, making a call just to see how things are going, helping when a legitimate need arises, coaching the girls' middle school volleyball team simply because you want to spend more time with the kids.

Pay careful attention to what Harry Beckwith says about sacrifice:

> Sacrifices tell [people] that you care, which makes them care more in return. Your sacrifice transforms the relationship. Now, you no longer are a service.

> You are *their* service. (2003, 249; italics in original)

2. Integrity

What do people experience when they call your school's business office? or try to contact a teacher? or attend a sporting event? or observe a teacher off campus? Integrity requires that each contact—however different in time, place, or content—produce a similar response: Wow, I'm impressed! If the experience sends a confusing variety of messages, some of them negative, then you can't expect people to think of your school as excellent. They may appreciate a particular teacher or coach or program, but they will find it hard to conclude that excellence characterizes your entire school unless your multifaceted performances match your promises of excellence.

3. Imagination and innovation

What makes a visit to Disney World such a wondrous experience? I suspect that the answers vary greatly. For me it is the reality that much of what one sees at Disney World began in the imagination of one man. Walt Disney did not bring his vision to life by himself; whole teams of remarkably creative people worked toward that goal, and therein lay a key to excellence. Disney, however, had the courage and imagination to see the remarkable contours of a vision no one else could see, and he then attracted and unleashed the kinds of people who would create the innovations that made his vision a reality.

I love it when I see glimpses of a similar kind of imagination and innovation in a Christian school. Let's be honest, however; not many people possess Walt Disney's imagination, but every school leader can still dream and then work hard at identifying and demolishing the roadblocks to excellence.

4. Discipline and persistence

Once during a question-and-answer session at a Shepherds' Conference, someone asked Dr. John MacArthur how he could accomplish so much, especially given the demands on his time. He gave this answer: "The key to good sermon preparation is simple. You've got to discipline yourself to stay at your desk in study, thought, and prayer, 30 to 35 hours—week in and week out. The greatest enemy most pastors face is their inability to resist the temptation to constantly step away from their work."

That answer sounds similar to the instruction the apostle Paul directs toward his young protégé Timothy: "Do not neglect the spiritual gift within you, which was bestowed on you…. Take pains with these things; be absorbed in them, so that your progress will be evident to all" (1 Timothy 4:14–15, NASB). Through discipline and persistence, you can keep focusing on what is crucial and keep working at making improvements instead of taking the easier course of action and chilling awhile.

I'm not talking about obsessive behavior; I'm talking about the quiet determination you should have to be better tomorrow than you are today and the disquiet you should feel when you begin to slip into the mind-set that says, "We're good enough." Satisfaction with your current performance paves the surest way to mediocrity. The pathway to excellence lies through the valley of discipline and persistence.

5. Trust

Whom do you trust? Why do you trust that person or those people? I must confess that the number of people I absolutely trust is relatively small. I trust my wife. In over forty years of marriage, she has proved time and again that she is worthy of my trust. I trust some friends. I can tell them anything, having absolute confidence that they will guard what I have told them. I also trust Lisa, the gal who cuts my hair.

Wow, that's a big leap—from wife and close friends to hairdresser. Why would I make that leap? It isn't that I trust Lisa with all my hopes and dreams. In reality, our conversations tend to focus on pretty superficial items: Where are you going on vacation? How 'bout those Broncos or Rockies or Nuggets? I don't trust Lisa with my life. I do, however, trust her with my hair. And not once in nearly ten years has she let me down. She always does her job with excellence, and that consistent excellence has built trust. Trust and excellence are inextricably tied together. Without excellence you cannot have trust, and where you have trust, you have excellence. Do your school parents trust you? How about your students? If not, why not?

6. Realism

Nothing derails innovative efforts, disrupts disciplined effort, or destroys trust faster than willingness by leaders to continually gloss over hard realities and ignore thoughtful observations. As Jim Collins notes, "Yes, leadership is about vision. But leadership is equally about creating a climate where the truth is heard and the brutal facts confronted. There's a huge difference between the opportunity to 'have your say' and the opportunity to be heard. The good-to-great leaders understood this distinction, creating a culture wherein people had a tremendous opportunity to be heard and, ultimately, for the truth to be heard" (2001, 74).

Achieving excellence will prove remarkably elusive, however, unless you are willing to take a long, hard, objective look at where you are as opposed to where you know you need to be. Objectivity is, however, elusive for all of us. In my experience it is helpful to seek insight from someone who will bring "a fresh set of eyes" to the task.

7. Passion

Excellence does not begin with a new laboratory filled with the latest equipment. Excellence begins when teachers refuse to allow a lack of resources to thwart them in pursuit of their passion. "Clients love passionate people and passionate businesses," notes Harry Beckwith, "because passion stimulates them—they feel it and feel better, too—because they know that passion produces great work" (2003, 260). Just think of the great teachers who influenced you. Stop for a moment and write down three things common to all of them. I'll bet you wrote *passion*: a passion for the subjects they were teaching and a passion for the students they were teaching. Passion fuels the drive for excellence.

Remember this. People may not easily see excellence; it often escapes detection. They cannot, however, mistake the passion for it. People enjoy spending time in the presence of genuine passion. Ask yourself these questions: Do people enjoy spending time in my presence? Do they sense my passion for the school I lead?

8. Exceptional people

Only excellent people can produce excellent results because only excellent people will pay the price necessary to achieve excellence. I hear something like the following retort whenever I talk about recruiting and retaining quality people: "We just don't have the money." If you really believe that such a retort has validity, let me go out on a limb and make a prophecy. You'll never build a school characterized by excellence. People—or as Jim Collins observes (2001), the right people in the right seats on the bus—are absolutely crucial to the success of your school and to your ability to make an impact on the lives of young people.

It is your responsibility as a leader to decide which qualities make for exceptional people. You must then relentlessly seek out those kinds of people to serve in your schools. And once you have them on your team, you must develop a decision-making process that unleashes the best qualities of those people as you seek to solve problems and deliver a truly excellent education.

A Final Question: What Are the Consequences of Mediocrity?

Is excellence really worth the effort? I think we sometimes benefit from asking ourselves what we lose if we fail to push on to excellence. Let's do a kind of reverse count-the-cost exercise and ask ourselves the following question: Beyond the obvious loss of students, what other real costs do we incur when we choose mediocrity over excellence?

We Diminish Our Impact

Mediocrity simply does not serve us well as we engage in the transforming process we call Christian schooling. Ask yourself these questions: If all that my students knew about the nature and character of God came from observing me and my staff, what conclusions do I think they would reach? Would they see the love, grace, forgiveness, patience, and holiness of God? Would they also see His creativity, His strategic thinking, His love of beauty, and His passion for excellence? If not, you are diminishing your ability to make an impact on their lives for Christ.

We Disease Our Hearts

Consider this thought from Jim Collins: "Yes, turning good into great takes energy, but the building of momentum adds more energy back into the pool than it takes out. Conversely, perpetuating mediocrity is an inherently depressing process and drains much more energy out of the pool than it puts back in" (2001, 208). That bit of modern business wisdom sounds similar to some ancient words from Solomon: "Hope deferred makes the heart sick" (Proverbs 13:12, NIV). Living in a situation in which poor quality describes the norm and excellence refers to only a distant, seemingly unattainable goal wears on a person's soul.

We Discredit Our Vocation

Listen to what the apostle Paul says to Timothy: "Be diligent to present yourself approved to God as a workman who does not need to be ashamed, accurately handling the word of truth" (2 Timothy 2:15, NASB). When we fail to achieve excellence as we fulfill our calling, we give people permission to discount not only our efforts but our holy vocation as well. Christian schools face enough challenges. We don't need to add to those challenges by presenting to the world an image of poor quality.

We Dilute Our Support

Excellence generates a response. Mediocrity earns a groan. If you don't believe me, just gauge the reaction of the crowd at a major-league sporting event or at a performance of a major touring company presenting a beloved musical or play. I've never seen a crowd cheer a game-losing error unless the visiting team was committing the error. Mediocre performances rarely earn standing ovations (except perhaps at an elementary school musical). I doubt you would often pay hard-earned money to sit through consistently poor performances.

I will continue to make this point throughout this book: people of wealth are not going to invest in mediocrity. Neither are they going to invest in your school in the hopes that it will one day change into a school of excellence. They will invest only when they see, in spite of whatever obstacles you face, a commitment to excellence that you actually have begun to deliver.

We Dishonor Our Lord

One of the most riveting events in the Old Testament evolved from King David's census of Israel. As a result of David's disobedience, Israel is suffering a great plague, and David sees a vision of the angel of the Lord holding a sword drawn to destroy Jerusalem. David responds with grief and repentance.

Following Gad's instructions, David sets out to purchase the threshing floor of Ornan for the purpose of building an altar on which to make a sacrifice to Yahweh. David approaches Ornan, whose response we can understand.

David is, after all, the king, a man of immense power. Ornan bows to David and says, "Take it for yourself; and let my lord the king do what is good in his sight. See, I will give the oxen for burnt offerings and the threshing sledges for wood and the wheat for the grain offering; I will give it all" (1 Chronicles 21:23, NASB).

David can have everything at no charge. That's a pretty good deal, one we would expect David to accept. He doesn't. He surprises us and teaches us an important lesson at the same time. He looks at Ornan kneeling on the ground and responds, "No, but I will surely buy it for the full price; for I will not take what is yours for the Lord, *or offer a burnt offering which costs me nothing*" (1 Chronicles 21:24; italics mine).

Excellence requires effort beyond the ordinary. We will not find it easy to achieve excellence, and we will certainly not find maintaining it easy once we've achieved it. Yet how could we offer less than our absolute best to our Lord? Listen again to the apostle Paul: "Whether, then, you eat or drink or whatever you do, do all to the glory of God" (1 Corinthians 10:31). Now ask yourself this question: When people settle their eyes on our school, do they see an unmistakable vision of God's glory, of God's excellence? If not, you need to ask yourself a second question: What must we do in order to do all things to the glory of God?

Conclusion

I know that any discussion about excellence can be frustrating. We sometimes find it difficult to define *excellence*, and we certainly face a challenge delivering it. However, we—especially those of us who call ourselves followers of Christ—show a serious lack of wisdom if we ignore the positive impact of excellence or the negative impact of mediocrity. We live in a world that demands excellence from those of us who provide goods or services, and we serve a Creator who is the very definition of excellence and who calls us to represent Him wisely and well. Excellence in pursuit of the person and purposes of Christ gives us a noble, worthwhile goal.

Chapter Six
Budgeting Basics:
Foundational Principles

I composed my first school budget on a legal pad. I found the budget a bit more complicated than my home budget, but not by much. I don't remember the numbers, but I do remember that it took just two pages to outline our school's income and expenses for the coming year. And like Charlie Brown's Christmas tree, it was a sorrowful sight to behold. *Inadequate* is an inadequate description. However, and here is the sad part, I could do no better given the preparation I had received, and I had recently earned a master's degree in school administration from a major state university.

Ten years later I replaced the legal pad with a spreadsheet. But although my financial reports looked more sophisticated, I still built them on much of the same flawed thinking that went into my first pen-and-paper budget. And therein lies the problem in many Christian schools. Few have qualified staff to shepherd the budget-development process, but because of the advent of more-accessible software the budget looks good, even if it is designed as poorly as the 1970 Chevrolet Vega.

Budget development requires more than a good tool; it requires competent counsel and a thorough understanding of what I call budgeting basics—all coupled with a sound process. We can easily find tools. We are swamped with tools. Software salespeople stand ready to assure you that their particular package will arm you with all you need to become the next budgeting guru. The only problem is that the claim is false. All budgeting tools lack two key ingredients: skill and judgment. If we have tools alone, we never have enough.

So if tools are not enough, what foundational principles must shape your efforts to build a sound financial future for your school? This chapter will answer that question. I have a modest goal for the chapter—Budgeting 101. I hope, however, that the contents will arm even the more experienced of you by providing you with a deeper understanding of foundational principles that should guide you in the budgeting process.

Reality Check

We must ground our budgeting process in reality. So before we jump into a discussion of these key principles, let's consider some real-life situations that illustrate what you may face as you approach your budgeting and financial-management responsibilities.

Scenario 1

Your parent-run school is relatively new, having existed less than ten years in a growing community populated by young professionals. Your primary competitors are the local public school, which has received several awards for quality programs, and a well-established parochial school sponsored by the largest Catholic parish in your area.

In the early years of your school, classes took place in a church facility. Six years ago the grandparents of one of the founders donated ten acres of land in a desirable area, and you began planning to build and relocate. An initial capital campaign generated enough gifts to justify moving ahead with the first phase of a multiphase plan. Your current facilities accommodate your current enrollment, but you must move ahead with further classroom construction to continue your growth. However, operational expenses are already accelerating beyond early estimates, and you paid for much of the cost of construction through a loan. You would find it difficult to service further debt, but you are facing significant pressure to increase enrollment to cover escalating costs. What are you going to do?

Scenario 2

Last year you watched with pride as the fortieth graduating class of your school celebrated the completion of high school. Forty years—it's hard to believe that much time has passed. The school is well-known, and it has made a major impact in your community. But a deteriorating local economy has led to a decrease in the area's population and to continually declining enrollment at your school. Significant growth will probably not take place even though the school board has agreed to a major new marketing initiative.

In addition, you have beyond-worn facilities and beyond-out-of-date instructional resources. You might be able to address one problem through a major push on your annual fund, but not two; and how will you bridge the gap in your operational budget if you divert annual-fund income to facility repairs?

Scenario 3

A recent bitter split in your sponsoring church has demoralized your staff and decimated your enrollment. You must make sharp cuts in staffing and programs to create any possible hope of keeping your doors open in the coming year. Worse, the reputation of the school has suffered because the public has heard about the feud, further decreasing the probability of achieving necessary enrollment goals.

You have a great facility, more than adequate for your current enrollment, but you've lost half your base. How will you cover that loss? Perhaps, as one of your board members has suggested, you should reconsider your enrollment policies. Perhaps you should open up enrollment to a more diverse student population.

Scenario 4

You are in the midst of five years of unprecedented growth. It all began even before the leaders of your sponsoring church asked the school board to consider a separation. No disagreements occurred; two expanding organizations simply needed access to static space. Since the amicable split, you have had to think more entrepreneurially, and you have come to see that necessity as a positive change. In fact, separation from the church has also allowed you to position the school as more of a community school, a situation that has led to greater support from a wider variety of area evangelical churches.

You have over time discovered, however, just how much your former sponsoring church actually subsidized the school's operational costs. The school has faced substantial increases in utility and maintenance costs, and now you must bear the expense of rent. Enrollment has increased, but so have expenses. What's the solution?

Perhaps you see yourself in one of these real-life situations, each of which requires a thoughtful response. The success of leadership teams in addressing such situations will largely depend on how well those teams understand and use the foundational principles I will unpack in the following pages.

Foundational Principles

I love Proverbs. In it we find ancient wisdom fully applicable to our modern times. Let me review what Derek Kidner writes: Proverbs "offers a key to life … The samples of behavior … are all assessed by one criterion, which could be summed up in the question, 'Is this wisdom or folly?' This is a unifying approach to life, because it suits the most commonplace realms as fully as the most exalted" (1964, 13). Thus I believe that as we study and read Proverbs we will uncover principles that fit closely with the best practices in the world of finance and budgeting. When key biblical principles and proven financial practices intersect, we should pay close attention.

Foundational Principle 1. Your operating budget should not rely on projected increases in enrollment, fund-raising efforts, or income from auxiliary services.

Proverbs 8:12 tells us, "I, wisdom, dwell with prudence, and I find knowledge and discretion" (ESV). In each of the above scenarios, we can easily see how any variety of external situations can produce nearly unbearable pressure on a school leadership team to build a budget that relies on such revenue increases. But Solomon reminds us that prudence offers us a better course of action than the wishful thinking that often characterizes budget deliberations.

Regardless of the scenario that describes your situation, I think you will be familiar with the following four questions that most boards repeatedly pose to their head of school before, during, and after the budgeting process. Note that each represents an attempt to reduce the upward pressure on tuition by either decreasing costs or increasing income in some way other than by increasing tuition:

- Can't we find a way to do it for less?
- Can't we find a way to recruit more students?
- Can't we raise more money from our donors?
- Can't we write a grant proposal and get some money from a foundation or a corporation?

All these questions reflect the same goal. Most boards are constantly seeking ways to reduce the price their schools must charge for educational services, thinking that lower costs will attract more students. Those boards are engaging in popular-but-flawed thinking, and we'll explore why later when we discuss how schools should set tuition.

If school boards cannot reduce costs enough to make a difference, they turn their attention toward increasing enrollment, increasing gift income, or more typically both. Having announced their intention, they make it an article of faith because, after all, they know with absolute certainty that God will meet their needs. We have touched on the misapplication of that theological principle. In short, when we make bad decisions, we—whether individuals or organizations—will probably suffer. We can't make poor decisions that are based on a flawed process and then expect God to ride in on the proverbial white horse to rescue us. Simply put, the promise of God's provision does not excuse lazy thinking and poor execution.

When our Lord sent His disciples out on their first independent mission, He didn't say, "Hey, when you get into trouble, give me a call and I'll be right over." He does promise His presence and His power. But in addition to His presence and power, He has given us specific gifts and the capacity to use those gifts with wisdom and discernment in solving even the most difficult problems. Thus He instructed His disciples, "I send you forth as sheep in the midst of wolves: *be ye therefore wise as serpents, and harmless as doves*" (Matthew 10:16, KJV; italics mine). In other words, Jesus told the disciples to figure it out.

God does provide. He provides all the attributes—such as wisdom, insight, and talent—that we need to fulfill His calling. Given those kinds of resources, we can make wise decisions, anticipate and respond to changing realities, solve perplexing problems, act with excellence, and continue as motivated and focused people even in the face of demanding difficulties.

We cannot respond to the challenges we experience, however, by helplessly shrugging our shoulders or fatalistically appealing to God's expected provision. So unless you have impeccable research that indisputably predicts a particular growth curve, you should never build your budget on the assumption of growth in enrollment or increases in annual giving and auxiliary income.

Foundational Principle 2. For funding and budgeting purposes, your budget must accurately differentiate between operational costs, program-enhancement costs, and capital-project costs.

We read in Proverbs 27:23–24, "Know well the condition of your flocks, and give attention to your herds, for riches do not last forever; and does a crown endure to all generations?" (ESV).

Jesus reminds us that the shepherd "calls his own sheep by name and leads them out" (John 10:3, NIV). Such an intimate understanding of a flock, the ability to differentiate between one sheep and another, makes possible the quality oversight that leads to success at caring for and building a flock. You need that same kind of careful insight when structuring a budget. You cannot treat all expenses the same; you must understand each within its own context.

For example, many understand the phrase "cost-based tuition" to mean a school must set tuition rates at a level sufficient to cover all costs related to operating the school. I don't fully agree with that understanding. Rather, I would argue that every school budget must distinguish between operational costs, program-enhancement (or program-development) costs, and capital-project costs. Further, every school must identify a separate revenue stream to fund each of those specific budget components. This topic will be discussed thoroughly in chapter 10.

Foundational Principle 3. Balanced budgets must include sufficient funding for not only the renewal and replacement of physical assets but also the continued professional development of faculty, administration, and staff.

Proverbs 21:5 informs us that "the plans of the diligent lead surely to abundance" (ESV). Sadly, however, I find that many school boards and leaders create financial plans that ultimately lead to serious challenges because those leaders simply do not account for the reality and necessity of setting aside resources to address inevitable needs that arise over time.

Think with me for a moment. What are the first categories in your budget you consider reducing or eliminating when facing a budget shortfall? Be honest. In my experience, efforts related to facilities and professional development suffer. After all, we rationalize, both of those areas fall under a category we label "nice but not necessary."

Here is the reality, however. Everything eventually breaks—everything. You may coax 250,000 miles out of that vehicle you bought ten years ago, but eventually you will have to replace your ride. And if you haven't been setting funds aside to help with the purchase, you will face one of two unfortunate choices. You will have to either finance the purchase or buy another "used to the point of worn" vehicle.

The first option burdens you with debt you don't need and probably can't afford. And you still have operational costs related to the purchase. The second option both requires the purchase of a less-than-ideal replacement and means months, perhaps years, of uncertainty and frustration over something as essential as your daily commute.

The same scenario will occur at your school if it fails to budget money for fixing all the things that will eventually break—everything from your air conditioners to your toilets to your roof to the panic hardware on your doors to the computer on your desk. Hear me on this. Everything eventually breaks, and the longer you wait, the greater the price you will pay when you finally must fix what has broken.

People break too, and in surprising and untimely ways that can create unexpected, expensive, and usually unnecessary problems. To keep that breaking from becoming a common occurrence at your school, you must invest in your staff in the same way you invest in your students. If you don't, you will soon find yourself losing your students, who are the ones funding your mission, and your staff, who are the ones delivering your mission.

The apostle Paul warns us not to become "weary in well doing" (Galatians 6:9, KJV) for good reason. We do—all of us. The antidote for weariness isn't all that complicated. People need a schedule that is reasonable, a task that is interesting, an income that provides for the basics, time for recreation, effective and timely encouragement, and continued intellectual, spiritual, and professional growth. If you ask someone to join your team, you have a responsibility in all those areas.

The call to teaching is noble. To pursue that calling with passion, grace, and integrity, however, can drain the intellectual, spiritual, and emotional reserves of even the strongest, most centered person. If our Lord saw the necessity of going aside regularly, how much more must we do so? Continued growth fostered by quality professional-development activities must never fall under the nice-but-not-necessary category of your budget.

Foundational Principle 4. Onetime, nonoperational expenses such as a construction project, major repairs of facilities, adoption of a new program, and purchases of new equipment should never burden a school's operational budget.

As Proverbs 22:7 tells us, "The rich rules over the poor, and the borrower is the slave of the lender" (ESV). One of the factors that make it difficult for schools to fully fund their operational costs from operational revenue relates directly to the violation of this principle. Consider the following illustrations:

- *Illustration 1.* The school year is about to begin when someone discovers a serious problem with the roof on the gymnasium. During recent heavy rains, leakage damaged the gym floor. A simple patch won't do. The school must replace the entire roof at a cost of $150,000. Without a reserve fund, how will the school pay for this emergency project?

- *Illustration 2.* You are out of space. After three straight years of enrollment growth, the school is using every square foot of its building, including the broom closet. It is time to build, so you launch a capital campaign. But of the $2 million in projected need, you raise only half. You don't want to borrow the money, but you do need the space, and you are afraid of what will happen if you don't move ahead with a much-publicized project. So what do you do?

In both illustrations, the schools will face strong temptation to borrow. In the first, the school does not want to approach a major donor to fund a crisis. All of us understand that hesitancy. The situation ends up diverting money from other crucial projects and sends a negative message about the school leadership's ability to plan for the unexpected. And how many schools have enough flexibility in their budget to divert $150,000 to what amounts to a major repair job?

In the second illustration, the school faces even-more-limited options. Either the school waits, or it borrows the money. Most schools will move ahead and find some kind of financing. They believe they can cover the cost of repayment by continued growth. That may happen, but they end up diverting their additional income from critical areas such as continued program development, increased compensation, professional development, scholarships, and the reserve fund. That trade never ends well because, as Solomon reminds us, the borrower has now become slave to the lender.

Would you dive into a deep, swiftly flowing river wearing a pair of heavy boots and a full field pack? Probably not. Few would survive. You would face an exhausting challenge simply staying afloat. When people are gasping for air, they are probably not thinking creatively or planning strategically. Debt service in an operational budget acts much the same way. I give the best financial advice I can to any school leader when I say this: don't burden your operational budget to fund capital projects.

Foundational Principle 5. You must make timely responses to changing budget realities.

Proverbs 22:3 instructs us, "The prudent sees danger and hides himself, but the simple go on and suffer for it" (ESV). We are talking about a simple concept. Any action or decision that increases the size of your budget requires a corresponding increase in revenue, and any decrease in budget revenue requires a corresponding decrease in the size of your budget. The principle doesn't change whether the increase or the decrease occurs as a result of a strategic decision or an unexpected event. Every school leader must learn to live within the reality of current budget constraints.

Many school leaders find themselves in trouble because they often wait too long to respond to changing financial realities. In fact, they often act like the gambler in Las Vegas who believes that sooner or later his or her luck has to change. The Christian school leader simply replaces luck with God. But God refuses to let us treat Him like a good-luck charm. Through Solomon God reminds us to be prudent—to look ahead and make wise decisions before the problem gets so out of hand that we are left with no good options. Yes, at times we can do nothing but cry out for God's help. But we face those kinds of situations only rarely.

Foundational Principle 6. Don't ignore the "uncontrollables."

In Proverbs 17:24 we read, "The discerning sets his face toward wisdom, but the eyes of a fool are on the ends of the earth" (ESV). In every budget-development process, your school will face both income and expense areas that you cannot predict with certainty to the point that making confident assumptions would show a lack of wisdom.

When dealing with those parts of your budget, you must exercise caution, track history carefully, challenge assumptions vigorously, and make estimates that err on the conservative side. Unfortunately, many of those responsible for budget development in Christian schools, like the fool, look at their situation unrealistically, believing they can reach the ends of the earth, so to speak, and thus end up setting "distant, godless, and unattainable goals" (Waltke 2005, 62). Consider the following categories of uncontrollables.

Annual giving

Once annual-giving efforts in a school become both mature and superb, annual giving tends to become less predictable and thus more uncontrollable for the following simple reasons:

- The school has little control over the amount of discretionary and super-discretionary income of school families. Family income can vary widely from year to year on the basis of job positions, job transfers, personal needs, family emergencies, performance of the stock market, performance bonuses, the general state of the economy, and any number of other issues.
- Changes may occur at the school in leadership, direction, programming, size, staffing, or something as simple as disappointment with a particular teacher or coach.
- Changes may occur in family situations such as through family size, graduation of a student, divorce, relocation, and illness.

In addition to these kinds of influences, annual funding is not typically going to grow in an upward arc indefinitely. Unless the support base of a school continues to increase annually in a substantial way, most schools will reach a ceiling of sorts in annual-giving revenue.

Planned giving

Your school may receive a large gift one year and nothing the following year, so you must give great care to how to build income from planned giving into your annual budget. The need for such care does not create a problem for most Christian schools simply because they have no planned-giving strategy.

In fact, only a small percentage of Christian schools have an effective annual-giving program, and even fewer have successfully launched and completed a quality capital campaign. Without a sound foundation in those areas, schools will find it difficult, probably impossible, to build effective planned-giving programs. As a result, Christian schools will suffer severe consequences.

Unfunded tuition

Imagine a year during which three, four, five, or more of your teachers retire or resign. Let's describe those teachers. They are older, more experienced, and probably second-income earners; they probably have children who have already graduated from school.

Now let's say you replace those teachers with younger teachers, all of whom have school-age children. Let's get specific and say you must replace four teachers with teachers who have a total of eight school-age children. And let's say that you provide discounts on tuition—from 50 to 100 percent—for children of teachers and staff as part of your compensation package. Do you see the challenge for budgeting?

Discounts are like wild cards in a game of chance. They can change the course of the game. And what holds true for your faculty holds true for any other target audience that receives a discount on tuition, whether you offer multichild discounts or pastoral discounts. You can't control, for example, the number of families who have three, four, or more students. Nor can you control the number of pastors who choose to send their children to your school. Because you can do neither, discounts are uncontrollable.

Auxiliary income and expenses

Auxiliary programs may vary greatly in size, nature, and complexity from one school to another, but most Christian schools operate auxiliary programs of some kind. Do you provide before- and after-school care for your students, a lunch program, or a summer camp program? If so, you operate an auxiliary program, and you must build your budget in such a way that you accurately reflect both income and expenses from such programs.

But it is important to note that you cannot always control auxiliary income and expenses. For example, families who sign their children up for your school's lunch program or summer camp program one year may not choose those options the next year. And the expenses for offering lunch or a camp can change significantly from year to year, especially in our unsettled economy.

Facilities upkeep

Many schools fail to build depreciation into their budgets. Schools cannot ignore, however, the fact that everything breaks—everything. And if (as is often the case) a school has cut corners when constructing its buildings, everything will break even sooner.

Those responsible for constructing a budget face an enormous challenge, especially if, as we've noted several times, the school has no history of building a reserve fund. Leaking roofs won't plug themselves, and failing air conditioners won't revive. Sooner or later you have to paint the walls, repair the dings, unclog the pipes, replace the flooring, or remove the asbestos. And here Murphy's Law applies: "If anything can go wrong, it will go wrong." That claim defines *uncontrollable* perfectly.

Technology

Do you remember the Apple IIe? If you do, you are giving away your age. At one time in the mid-1980s, people considered the Apple IIe the cutting edge of educational technology. Remember the IBM Selectric typewriter? How about the first Texas Instruments calculators or the slide rules they began to replace?

My point is simple. We have been riding the rapids of technological innovation for more than thirty years, and we have paid a staggering financial cost for this thrill ride. Technological innovation probably isn't going to slow down, and you simply can't jump ship. Your community and your school parents perceive a connection between technology and excellence.

You have probably noticed that the shelf life of new technology is decreasing. Schools will face increasing costs to stay current technologically. And we've touched only on the hardware. What did you pay for your first administrative software package? How about the price tag on the latest upgrade? In this area of your budget, you are definitely facing an uncontrollable.

Insurance

I recently visited a school in Florida that is facing a 50 percent increase in the price it must pay for a policy to insure its facilities. In a single year the cost has risen from $150,000 to $225,000. Given the number of recent hurricanes and the prediction of an increasing number of powerful storms over the next twenty years, the school's current rate may look like a bargain in ten years.

You may not be leading a school in hurricane-prone Florida or earthquake-vulnerable California, but the cost of building supplies is rising at a staggering rate (Facilitiesnet.com 2007), so every school everywhere faces similar challenges. And facilities insurance is just the beginning of the problem. Go back and track what has happened to the cost of providing medical insurance for your staff. Shocking, isn't it?

Conclusion

I have been trying to drive home a simple point. Those responsible for developing and managing a household budget face a daunting task made even more difficult by realities over which they have little or no control. Now magnify the size of the challenge a thousandfold and you'll be describing your school budget. Because of the magnitude of the challenge, you absolutely must employ a sound, utterly realistic budgeting process that accurately assesses the true cost of providing a quality education in these unsettled days.

In the second half of this book, I want to clearly outline a sound process for developing a realistic budget for your school. So let's get started.

Chapter Seven
The Budgeting Team

Do you often stay at the end of a movie to watch the credits roll? Probably not. Your time is too valuable, and you don't seem to have any reason to invest the time unless you have a friend or a family member who served as part of the production crew. You may want to try doing so sometime, however. You will gain a greater appreciation for just how complex moviemaking can be. The list of names and job titles seems as endless as it does confusing. Director you understand, but best boy? And just what does a key grip do?

I found those names essentially meaningless until I did some research. Let me summarize what I learned. Each of those people has a specific role to play. And each person understands that role—what it is, what it isn't, and how all the various pieces fit together into a remarkable whole. It may look complicated to the uninitiated, but those on the set have absolute clarity. And never, not even once, does the key grip or the assistant key grip ever presume to sit in the director's chair and give advice on how best to film a scene—not unless his or her real career goal involves collecting unemployment benefits.

Unfortunately, we don't always see that same kind of clarity in the budget-development process in Christian schools. In this chapter I hope to reduce the ambiguity that often plagues school administrators and school board members regarding the distinct yet complementary roles each must play during the budget-development and budget-oversight processes.

This chapter reflects secondary purposes as well. First of all, I want to help stop the carnage that can occur when school leaders and board members clash over roles that are misunderstood—or even sometimes purposefully manipulated to ensure control over financial decisions or to maintain inappropriate power.

In either case, misunderstanding or manipulation, good people suffer great harm, school reputations are tarnished, and the cause of Christ is damaged in the eyes of students, parents, the church, and the community. That price is too high and unnecessary to pay for ignorance of a simple process. I can't control the motives of people, but I hope this book will provide helpful information regarding a process that in good hands can produce a quality result.

Second, I want to address the reality that schools at times need to adjust standard operating procedures. Some situations will require a modified approach. Usually those situations relate to new schools or to schools in transition, but on occasion some modifications may make sense because of the particular nature of a school's governance.

I believe that good people will usually produce positive results if you give them quality tools, clear direction, and the right motivation. Having noted the premise that you must put together the right team, I think the information in this chapter will give you the best approach to an extraordinarily important job.

The Budgeting Team: How the Board and the Chief School Officer Relate

If we are going to achieve clarity regarding the complementary roles of the board and the chief school officer (CSO) in the budgeting process, we must first understand the structural relationship between the board and the CSO. On this topic much ink and much blood have been spilled. (See appendix A, Resources for Board Leadership, at the end of this book.)

Something particularly American complicates the discussion. We are forever caught between our rather romantic idealization of the solitary, visionary leader and our democratic, everyone-must-have-a-voice impulses. I think we tend to take those cultural inclinations to our conversation about governance in Christian schools.

Our confusion over the meanings of the words *purpose, mission,* and *vision* further complicates the discussion. We discussed the differences between the *purpose* and *mission.* Now we need to distinguish between *mission* and *vision* because the difference has huge implications for any school's budget and greatly affects our understanding of the relationship between the board and the CSO.

Resolving the Problem of Conflicting Vision

How many times have you heard someone say something such as this: "If we ever hope to become a school known for excellence, we must …"? We must have a better fine arts program, a better math program, better technology, a better library, a better gymnasium, a better biology lab, or a full-time development person, registrar, or staff chaplain. We could create an almost endless list, and there are passionate advocates for every point.

We have difficulty understanding the nature of vision and the role the CSO plays in both discovering and delivering a vision, and that difficulty complicates the issue of conflicting visions. Boards are important, but no matter how well a board does its job, it cannot make an organization great. A great board can and should facilitate greatness, encourage greatness, and help fund greatness, but it cannot create greatness. Instead, the head of school and his or her team have the responsibility for creating greatness. A board can, however, frustrate greatness by acting inappropriately. This mistake it must avoid.

I believe that vision is born in the heart of a leader. Great leaders constantly think about the future—not just in terms of time but in terms of what an organization can become. Board members certainly think about the future, and they want to see the school improve, but they simply do not spend the time pondering the future in the same way as the head of school—nor can they, in all reality, spend the time. Most board members have a job, and they are expected to invest time, energy, and creative thought in performing that job well.

The purpose explains why a school exists. The mission describes what a school is supposed to be doing. The vision drives purpose and mission by helping people see the school's potential impact. Thus the right vision can energize people, inspire people, establish a sound standard by which to shape decisions, and build a bridge from current reality to a preferred future.

If what I've said about mission and vision and about board roles and leadership roles is true, we have to consider certain implications. For example, we have to ask ourselves, Who should be the primary driver in discussions related to vision—the board or the CSO? Or can we perhaps find another way to approach the issue of vision? This discussion is especially pertinent because vision always has a price tag, and that price tag will eventually affect budget discussions. Here are some thoughts to consider as you work through this issue as a team consisting of the board, the CSO, and the staff.

As guardian of the trust, the board bears the primary responsibility for defining what is nonnegotiable about the school. As we discussed, these nonnegotiables consist of beliefs, purpose, mission, values, and outcomes.

Note that I have not included the word *vision* in that list of nonnegotiables. Rarely does an organization change its beliefs or its purpose or its mission or its values or its outcomes. When it does change in those areas, it changes into an entirely different organization, committed to entirely different goals. Think Harvard. It drifted because it rejected its core set of beliefs about the nature of God. The members of the governing body changed what they believed and thus negotiated away a nonnegotiable.

Organizational vision can, however, change over time without surrendering what is nonnegotiable. I have a friend, Dr. George Janvier, who serves in Nigeria under the auspices of SIM, a mission agency that for years engaged in planting new churches. Today SIM focuses on equipping national leaders to both plant and pastor churches. So Dr. Janvier does not travel the country as an evangelist or a church planter. He heads a seminary that fulfills SIM's new vision to develop a generation of national leaders for the church in Africa.

SIM's concern about planting new churches and strengthening mature churches has not changed. But SIM does not primarily invest in missionaries who have a vision to plant churches. Instead, it focuses on equipping national leaders who will plant churches and strengthen them. Here are some additional thoughts on vision I'd like you to consider.

God is the author of vision. Moses didn't call Moses to a vision of leading the people of Israel from slavery to freedom. God did. Abraham didn't call Abraham to a vision of producing a called-apart nation. God did. Noah didn't call Noah to build an ark. God did. David didn't call David to the throne. God did. And what of the apostles? What of Paul? What of Augustine and Luther and Calvin? And what about you? God calls; we respond, or we don't. But it is always God who initiates the conversation.

Leaders typically are the first to discover God's vision. You may be thinking, "Ah, I think I may have you on this point, Dr. Pue. After all, could Noah be called a leader? And as for Moses, he may have been a leader at one time, but he spent forty years tending another man's sheep in the wilderness. So isn't it possible that someone other than the core leader can discover God's vision for a particular organization?" Of course. I simply believe that typically the person to whom leadership has been entrusted, if that person is thinking as a leader should be thinking and praying as a leader should be praying, is more likely to sense and see God's vision for a particular ministry.

Discovery and confirmation of a vision typically take place as a result of a sound process, not sudden perception. The danger, of course, is that the leader will grow impatient and try to force certain decisions on the board, an action that is inappropriate and unwise. Mature leaders will always allow testing of their ideas and thoughts. A strategic-planning process provides that testing. If the vision that has formed in the heart of a leader has come from God, a sound planning process will confirm that vision. A leader has nothing to fear when a team of godly people humble themselves to seek the mind of God.

The Spirit of God will not lead in multiple directions. When those serving in leadership do not have unity concerning an organization's future, the problem does not lie with God's Spirit but with the motives and personal agendas of the leadership team. Then the team members need to back away from the process and seek wise counsel.

People cannot fully own or generously support a vision they do not thoroughly understand. This reality partly explains why schools should engage in a sound planning process coupled with a comprehensive communication strategy. A strong task force not only will add wisdom and insight to the process but also will lend its credibility to both the process itself and the initiatives that emerge.

If the school indeed has a sound process, the individual members of the task force will also serve as influencers in helping others more fully understand the rationale for new strategic initiatives that form the basis for the school's vision. A school leadership team can never impose a vision. People must own a vision. To own it, people must understand it, and once they understand it, it must make sense. Task force members in a sense become both heralds and ambassadors of the vision that emerges from the planning process.

Establishing the Role of the Board

The series of workshops I teach entitled Guarding the Trust explores the responsibilities of a board in leading a Christian school. That title comes from a phrase the apostle Paul used in his personal correspondence with the young and apparently beleaguered pastor of the church at Ephesus. Paul writes, "O Timothy, *guard what has been entrusted to you*, avoiding worldly and empty chatter and the opposing arguments of what is falsely called 'knowledge' " (1 Timothy 6:20, NASB; italics mine).

Only a few decades had passed since the death and resurrection of Jesus, but during that brief time false teachers seeking to distort the gospel for their own benefit were propagating misleading ideas. In such an environment it was a pastor's responsibility to ensure the integrity of the gospel, not only to keep it whole and untainted by any idea contrary to the truth but also to deposit that truth into the hearts and lives of the next generation of leaders (see 2 Timothy 2:1–2).

The language that Paul uses comes directly from the world of banking. In the ancient world, as is true today, a person could entrust to a banker's care personal items of great value: money, gems or precious metals, works of art, or even a piece of property. The board of a Christian school functions in much the same way as those early bankers.

To the board is entrusted the most valuable aspect of any school: its non-negotiable core—that is, its beliefs, purpose, mission, values, and outcomes. The board holds that trust on behalf of the owners of the school, whether a parent organization, a particular church, or a coalition of churches. In guarding the trust on behalf of those owners, the board must carry out two main tasks of ensuring and one of protecting.

Ensuring

First, the board must ensure that the school in all its policies and practices continues to represent the nonnegotiable core, which thus must govern the school. At the very beginning, therefore, when working through a strategic-planning process with a school, I require the task force to complete the essential first step—revisit and validate what it considers nonnegotiable.

I believe a planning process that begins with a search for a vision potentially puts the school at risk. Vision is dynamic, and being dynamic is a good thing. But unless a school leadership team takes great care, a compelling vision can subtly alter the landscape of the school, in effect changing its very core. The same thing can occur during a budgeting process. Thus the board must ensure that all budgeting decisions remain consistent with and in support of the core.

Second, the board must ensure the school's continued fiscal health. It does so in two ways. The board must develop effective financial policies that protect the school from unwise decisions by itself or by the head of school, and the board must work diligently to build long-term financial strength into the school through encouraging and supporting effective resource-development efforts. Even the most exceptional team in the world will fail if its school has insufficient resources to maintain and advance the mission.

One of the first questions a foundation or a private donor poses when approached with a funding request is this: What is your board doing personally to fund this project? Unless the entire board is participating at a generous level, there is little probability of a positive response to any request, proposal, or grant. Resource development always, always, always begins from the center of an organization—meaning the board, key leadership, faculty, and staff—and then works outward.

That order makes sense, doesn't it? Why should a complete stranger support your efforts if you are unwilling to do so yourself? No one should serve on a Christian school board unless he or she has demonstrated a thorough understanding of and support for the school's nonnegotiable core. Nor should anyone serve who has not demonstrated a willingness to financially support the school regularly.

On these points I am uncompromising. I've heard all the arguments: this is a great parent who just doesn't have the money, this person has a lot of influence in the community, this is the pastor of the largest church in the area, we need someone with legal—or accounting or building or some other kind you can think of—expertise on our board. And on and on it goes. If you fall for those arguments, sooner or later you will regret your decision.

The following should characterize the board members you choose:
- They possess impeccable character. Use 1 Timothy 3:1–7, 2 Timothy 2:1–25, and Isaiah 32:1–8 as guides in deciding whom you ask to serve.
- They show significant ability as apologists, and they are willing and winsome advocates for Christian schooling. Ask only people who understand the biblical, educational, and cultural rationale for Christian schooling and who can and will discuss and defend that rationale in an articulate and winsome manner.
- They demonstrate public passion for your school through a generous investment of time, talent, and treasure. A person who seeks influence apart from giving has, at heart, a passion for power, not a passion of purpose. Avoid those people at all cost.
- They exhibit a passion for lifelong learning. Find people who demonstrate teachableness. Carefully study Proverbs 18 and you will better understand the profile of the kind of people you want on your board.
- They bring with them useful skills, experiences, information, or relationships. These resources can greatly benefit your school but only when the prospective members hold the other qualities in abundance.

In response to that list, I hear a typical argument that begins with a phrase similar to this: "You must be kidding. We have maybe two people in our entire constituency who meet those qualifications." I have a simple answer to that objection. Begin with a board of two. Then make it a priority of the board to identify or develop additional board members.

Then I hear this corollary objection: "Our bylaws require seven board members, so sometimes we have to compromise a bit on the personal qualifications to meet that goal." I have an equally simple answer to that objection. You "need" two legs to walk. So what do you do if cancerous tumors fill one of those legs? You either kill the tumors or remove the leg. Two legs are better than one unless one leg contains something that will eventually kill you. Forgive the comparison, but bad board members can have an effect like that of cancerous tumors. Eventually those members will cripple or even kill an organization.

Bylaws and constitutions are important documents. If you ignore them, you are usually acting unwisely. But nothing will demoralize, diminish, or destroy an organization faster than filling leadership positions with the wrong people. Don't do it.

Protecting

So besides its tasks of ensuring, what does the board do to carry out its responsibility of guarding the trust? The board protects the school's reputation and image. This part of the board's responsibility covers a lot of important territory. For instance, when a board develops policies regarding executive limitations, it does so in part because of its concern about how a CSO's behavior might reflect on the organization.

Some of those limitations wisely relate to fiscal policy. For example, few things will tarnish the image of a school faster than failure to pay bills on time. And rightfully so. The Scriptures clearly command us to keep our promises. Weak or incompetent or unfocused leaders can quickly put their schools at financial risk either because those leaders don't do their job right or because their poor leadership efforts limit enrollment and diminish support. The board must ensure that this financial risk doesn't occur, not through directly managing but through both developing wise financial policies and appropriately overseeing the head of school.

Budget Responsibilities

Now, how do we translate all that information into action? What are the specific responsibilities of the board regarding the budget? The board has primary responsibility for six areas: the board (1) sets appropriate limitations, (2) approves executive assumptions, (3) approves compensation structures, (4) sets tuition rates, (5) approves the final budget, and (6) ensures appropriate oversight.

I have used care in choosing the action words in each of these responsibilities. Note, for example, the significant difference between the phrases "*ensures* appropriate oversight" and "*provides* appropriate oversight." I have chosen my words on the assumption that the board should never do administrative work. The board should never function as a superadministrator and should never do the work of the CSO.

If the board functions as a superadministrator, two bad results always occur. First, that kind of behavior will eventually drive away a strong leader. Second, that kind of behavior will inevitably attract a weak leader.

1. Sets appropriate limitations

The first thing God did after creating Adam was to give him a job:

> "Be fruitful and multiply, and fill the earth, and subdue it; and rule over the fish of the sea and over the birds of the sky and over every living thing that moves on the earth." Then God said, "Behold, I have given you every plant yielding seed that is on the surface of all the earth, and every tree which has fruit yielding seed; it shall be food for you...."

> Then the Lord God took the man and put him into the garden of Eden to cultivate it and keep it. The Lord God commanded the man, saying, "From any tree of the garden you may eat freely; but from the tree of the knowledge of good and evil you shall not eat, for in the day that you eat from it you will surely die."

> Then the Lord God said, "It is not good for the man to be alone; I will make him a helper suitable for him." Out of the ground the Lord God formed every beast of the field and every bird of the sky, and brought them to the man to see what he would call them; and whatever the man called a living creature, that was its name. (Genesis 1:28–29, 2:15–19, NASB)

Notice with me several interesting components of this job description:

- It is enormous in scope. God gave Adam responsibility for the entire creation. I'd say Adam had a big job.
- It is spare in its language. Only a few key verbs explain the job: *be fruitful, multiply, fill, subdue, rule, cultivate,* and *keep*. It seems to me that great detail in the head of school's job description clearly indicates that you have little confidence in the person you are calling as the leader of your school.
- It is clear in its limitations. Do this; don't do this. If you want to do the best thing you can ever do for a leader, be clear about the nature of the job and be equally unambiguous about any limits related to the leader's job.
- It is confident in its provision. God details not only the job expectations but also the resources He is making available to Adam. This point is key. Never call a person to a job for which you do not provide appropriate resources. And notice as well that God acknowledges that Adam needs a helper.
- It is certain in its choice. The naming of the animals is an important event. In it we learn a key principle. If you call someone to a task, let that person do it. God could have easily given names to all the animals, but He chose to step aside and let Adam do the task to which God called him. Don't call a leader and then do his or her job. If the leader lets you do that, that person is not a leader.

The board's first responsibility in the budgeting process is simple. Develop policies that set clear boundaries for the CSO. Build a fence and hang this sign on it: "Beyond this point you may not go." If you want some specific ideas on finance policies, purchase and read either *Christian School Board Governance* (Keenan 2007) or *Reinventing Your Board* (Carver and Carver 1997).

2. Approves executive assumptions

Approving assumptions requires a high degree of faith in the CSO and in his or her ability to make accurate predictions related to projected expenses and income. This need for faith may explain why so many boards show reluctance about backing away too far during the budget-development process. Yet back away a board must.

If a board does not have sufficient confidence in the CSO, the board should take one of three actions. If it took the first and best action, the board would hire a CFO (chief financial officer) to work as the CSO's right arm in the budgeting process—a good idea anyway. In the budgeting process the CSO and the CFO should work together as a team. If it chose the second action, the board would replace the CSO with someone who has a greater level of financial savvy. If the board can reassign the CSO to a position that better connects talent to task, the board could do so. If not, the board will need to replace that person. The board could choose a third option by finding a volunteer CFO who is willing to donate time to help the CSO develop a sound predictive model for both expenses and income. If the CFO is serving as a board member, he or she must step away from the board position.

The CSO, not the board, has the responsibility of developing assumptions regarding both expenses and income. The board has the responsibility of questioning the CSO on the design of all predictive models until the board finds the validity of those models satisfactory. At that point the board should approve the assumptions that will form the basis for the budget.

3. Approves compensation structures

My friend and colleague Mickey Bowdon once described the role of the board and the role of the CSO in budget development in the following simple language: "The role of the CSO is to define excellence and to give it a price tag. The role of the board is to decide how much excellence it wants to buy." If Mickey's statement is true, and I believe it is, it has significant implications for the budget-development process because it requires the board to release to the CSO all authority and responsibility for designing a budget that can indeed lay the foundation for excellence.

If, as I discussed earlier, people are the key to excellence, then the CSO is fulfilling a key responsibility when recruiting and retaining those people. To do that well, the CSO must have the freedom to first describe the kinds of people to be recruited except in those areas restricted by policy limitations, and then the CSO must have the freedom to establish a reasonable framework, again within policy limitations, for recruiting and retaining quality teachers. That framework would of necessity include compensation levels.

In most schools the board sets both hiring guidelines and compensation levels for staff. When the board does so, it is assuming a key leadership prerogative and usurping the CSO's role. The board has one employee, the CSO. The board, therefore, designs one job description and develops one compensation package.

The CSO cannot, however, establish any salary schedule he or she desires. The board still has enormous control over the shape of the budget because the board can establish policies that limit the CSO's freedom in setting salaries or hiring new faculty and staff. But once the board has put those policies in place, the board must give the CSO the freedom to develop the compensation structure.

4. Sets tuition rates

Remember this mantra: the CSO defines excellence and gives it a price tag; the board decides how much excellence it wants to buy. One of the key tools the board has at its disposal in this regard is its authority to set tuition rates. Once the board sets tuition rates, they become a default policy limitation requiring the CSO to build a budget within certain parameters.

The most intense level of discussion will occur at this point, both within the board and between the board and the CSO. Remember that both the board and the CSO must concern themselves with excellence, even though the CSO has been specifically tasked with defining excellence and giving it a price tag.

The board must concern itself with excellence for several reasons. First of all, it has a responsibility to the owners of the trust and to the school's constituents to ensure that everything related to the school takes place with excellence. Second, it has a responsibility to the one called to lead the school, the CSO. Remember, God not only gave Adam a job but provided enough resources to fulfill the requirements of the job as well. Third, the board bears the responsibility of representing the ultimate owner of the school, Jesus Christ. Since Christ is the very definition of excellence, if we act with mediocrity in any way, we are blurring His image, dishonoring His person, and diminishing His work.

I am not suggesting that a CSO should have the freedom to build any budget he or she desires without taking reality into account. I do believe, however, that boards often sanction mediocrity simply because they give in to fear and refuse to set tuition at a level sufficient to achieve excellence.

5. Approves the final budget

Although the board does not build the budget, it must give final approval to the details in the budget that the CSO and his or her team constructs. This is not typically a decision made in a single, brief meeting. In one sense the board is involved in every aspect of the budgeting process.

Let's review. The board through its policies sets clear financial boundaries for the CSO. The board then examines and approves all assumptions regarding expenses and income provided by the CSO. The board also approves any new compensation levels for faculty and staff and establishes the key funding mechanism for the school by setting new tuition rates. Because of that level of familiarity with and access to the budget, the board should be in position to ask pertinent questions about the specifics of the budget and give approval in the course of a single meeting. If not, the process has failed at some point.

6. Ensures appropriate oversight

If the board has done all I have outlined above, then appropriate oversight requires that the board do two, on occasion three, things. First, the board must arrange for an annual audit. Both words are key; *annual* indicates every year, and *audit* indicates someone from outside the organization who has the appropriate qualifications. An annual audit is not a nice thing to do: it is an essential thing to do.

It does cost money to do an audit. But without an audit, the board cannot adequately fulfill its responsibility to ensure appropriate budget oversight. An audit does, however, provide the basis for helping a school increase its income because nearly every foundation, corporation, or individual that might show interest in responding to a grant, proposal, or request for funding will ask for three years' worth of audited financials—not all foundations, corporations, or individuals, but most. When a board fails to require annual audits, it fails not only in its oversight obligation but in its resource-development obligation as well.

Second, require monthly financial reports. The board can dramatically reduce the reporting time by disciplining itself to ask two key questions: "Have any of the expense assumptions changed?" and "Have any of the income assumptions changed?" If the answer to both of those questions is no, the board has completed the financial-report portion of the meeting. How long did it take you to read this paragraph? That's all the time you need for a financial report.

If the CSO answers yes to either question, the CSO should have already developed a course of action that addresses any changes in the assumptions. If the answer to those questions is yes month after month, the board knows the CSO has inadequate knowledge, skills, or talent to provide wise fiscal leadership for the school.

Establishing the Role of the Chief School Officer

To use a construction metaphor, a school board carries out an approval function similar to that of a local zoning commission, whereas the CSO serves as a construction manager. The board limits and approves. The CSO designs and constructs. In terms of specific responsibilities, the CSO (1) represents the faculty and staff to the board and the board to the faculty and staff; (2) develops, with appropriate faculty and staff participation, the assumptions on which the budget will be built; (3) ensures equity in the distribution of resources; (4) proposes the compensation structure; (5) provides appropriate oversight and management of the budget; and (6) makes the board aware of changes in any budget assumptions and recommends any necessary budget revisions.

1. Represents the faculty and staff to the board and the board to the faculty and staff

The CSO plays the role of mediator—one of the most challenging roles he or she will ever play—and must do so on two levels: first of all as the mediator between the board and the staff, and second as the mediator between each element of the staff. Let's consider three of the most important reasons the CSO will find this task difficult: conflicting visions, conflicting versions of reality, and internal or external power struggles.

Conflicting visions. We've discussed the issue of conflicting visions as it relates to the board and the head of school. Staff members, however, can have conflicting visions as well. A wise leader will seek insight and wisdom from his or her team, but a leader who abdicates his or her crucial role in vision development ceases to lead.

Leaders must lead, and in fulfilling one of their primary obligations, they must initiate and drive the conversation about the best direction to take in pursuing an organization's purpose and mission. Staff can shape thinking and suggest tactics, but they cannot be the drivers. If at any time a staff member, no matter how key, can no longer support either the mission or the vision of an organization, that person should take the only honorable course of action—resign.

Conflicting versions of reality. The perspective we bring to a conversation largely drives the reality we see. The wise leader will constantly seek insight and wisdom from key people—staff members, board members, and key constituents—but in the end the leader must decide what is real at that moment for the organization.

Often during my years as a head of school, a faculty member or a parent who wanted to influence my decisions would approach me. For the most part I appreciated the spirit of these people and often saw value in their ideas. However, they typically lacked perspective. Yes, it would be great to make a certain change in the elementary school or to purchase a particular resource for the middle school or to add a particular program in the high school. In isolation from other relevant facts, each idea had merit. Add in those other facts, however, and suddenly everything changes.

As the head of school, I had the job of ensuring that all relevant facts shaped every decision. In so doing, I knew that on occasion I would disappoint someone by choosing A instead of B. But leaders are always making tough choices between competing options. Failure to fulfill this responsibility not only puts an organization at risk financially and "missionally" but also eventually diverts the energy and resources necessary to pursue the organization's vision.

Internal or external power struggles. I wish we could ignore the sad reality of politics. We can't. Painful personal experience has taught me how great an impact politics can have on an organization, even one committed to biblical ideals. Here we face a huge topic, far beyond the scope of this book. I will, however, make a couple of observations.

First, the leader of any organization must remain aware of what people think, and that awareness will exist only if the leader gets out of his or her office and talks with people. A leader must continually take the organization's pulse. Most of that pulse taking will occur in nonformal settings. Questionnaires and surveys have their place, but nothing will substitute for face-to-face conversation.

Second, the leader of any organization must act at the first sign of trouble or discontent. If a leader learns of a staff member or a board member who is publicly lobbying for a particular position or direction that contradicts the school's clearly understood mission, values, or vision, then the leader must address that person personally and privately if it is a staff member or must speak to the board chair if that person is a board member.

Great leaders want to encourage divergent points of view. In private meetings a bit of constructive conflict is healthful, even necessary, and often it will lead to a better idea or solution. But divergent points of view expressed in public will only harm the organization.

2. Develops, with appropriate faculty and staff participation, the assumptions on which the budget will be built

Budget assumptions fall under two categories: expense assumptions and income assumptions. By assumptions I do not mean uninformed guesses about what expenses or income might be. Instead, the CSO makes best guesses on the basis of appropriate research, a sound process, and accurate historical data. The head of school—not the board—has the responsibility, working with his or her management team, to create all the assumptions that form the basis for the budget.

Obviously some situations call for exceptions. In a smaller school, for example, the task of developing assumptions might fall almost exclusively on the head of school. But even in a small school, staff will play a role in tracking retention numbers, on which the CSO will partially base the enrollment numbers. Staff in a small school will also help determine the need for instructional resources.

Smaller schools also tend to face another problem in budgeting and finance: the CSO's lack of experience, lack of preparation, or both. If so, it sometimes makes sense for qualified board members to participate more in budget development. A better solution, at least for the long haul, is to ensure that the head of school receives appropriate training in the basics of budgeting and finance. Budgeting in a small school is seldom complicated except by a lack of resources. I write this book with the hope that it will serve as a resource in equipping heads of schools and boards for their respective responsibilities in the budgeting process.

3. Ensures equity in the distribution of resources

Many schools do not face the problem of ensuring resource equity. Those schools have limited programs, and resources barely cover basic operational costs. As a school grows in numbers and complexity, however, conflicts over the best use of limited resources can create more of a challenge. The way many schools connect fund-raising activities to particular projects exacerbates the problem.

Fund-raising, like every other component of a school, should result from agreed-upon strategic initiatives. When those initiatives do not drive fund-raising, the impact of a popular teacher or an influential parent or board member can easily divert resources from genuinely crucial projects to personal projects. The same can occur during the normal budgeting process. Without a sound frame of reference, a passionate presentation or a political maneuver can easily but inappropriately direct resources to a private rather than a strategic end. The head of school must ensure that those diversions do not occur.

On occasion a particular donor will make a restricted gift to fund a particular project. In most cases a school would be acting unwisely if it refused such a gift, though at times such a restricted gift could fundamentally divert a school from its mission and vision. What would you do, for example, if a donor agreed to fund construction of a new football field and then further to fund the operational cost of the program for three years?

If in your strategic-planning process you had identified adding football as a key initiative, then you'd probably rejoice at such a gift. If, however, the school had a vision to develop a strong fine arts program, you'd face a more difficult decision.

Who makes that choice? I would argue that the strategic plan of the school should drive that choice. I would also argue that the head of school should serve as the primary decision maker in such a situation since the head of school has the responsibility of implementing the strategic plan. Given the magnitude of the gift I just described, clearly the board should also engage in the decision, but if the board shifts the priorities of the school in response to a major gift, that shift could result in some serious problems, including resignation of the head of school.

In the course of a normal budgeting process, however, I would argue that the head of school holds the most responsibility for tough calls when those calls entail distribution of resources. The head of school may—in fact should—seek input from key staff, but in the end he or she must make the decision and take responsibility for it.

4. Proposes the compensation structure

Remember, the head of school has a responsibility to describe excellence and determine the means necessary to achieve excellence. The right staff members are absolutely crucial to delivering excellence. The right staff, however, always come with a price tag. Therefore, the head of school must communicate the following to the board: this is what it will cost for us to hire the kind of staff we need to deliver the kind of program that we envision and that we have promised to our constituency.

To do his or her job well, the head of school must carefully research teacher compensation in the school's area. School leaders simply cannot ignore market realities, nor can they ignore the biblical principles we explored in chapter 3. By the way, I strongly believe that appropriate performance benchmarks should influence salary levels. I don't believe money is the primary motivator for teachers in a Christian school, but I do believe that rewarding people for exceptional performance says to them appropriately, "Thank you for an exceptional job."

Many businesses use a compensation structure that takes into account numerous variables in determining individual salaries. In an educational setting those variables should certainly include academic achievement, years of experience, and level of responsibility. But in addition, school leadership should find a way to reward creativity, commitment, and performance. The head of school should lead in the process of developing those more subjective measurements.

5. Provides appropriate oversight and management of the budget

The board is accountable to all constituents for the fiscal health of the school. The head of school wears that bull's-eye in relation to the board. Thus the head of school holds the full responsibility for developing and daily overseeing the budget; both management functions fall fully on the management team.

When I teach on this topic, school board members most frequently respond, "Dr. Pue, we have a fine administrator who has a strong understanding of educational philosophy and instructional strategy. Our administrator does not, however, have a sufficient understanding of finance to either build or oversee the school budget." I give the following simple response, which I gave previously in this chapter: "If the head of school is not sufficiently equipped for the job, make sure he or she receives appropriate training and, if possible, professional assistance."

6. Makes the board aware of changes in any budget assumptions and recommends any necessary budget revisions

Over time, projected expense or income assumptions will inevitably require revision. No matter how good the data, unexpected events occur. A major employer in the community lays off a couple of thousand workers, and your enrollment drops; or your insurance carrier announces significant, unanticipated increases in premiums, and your expenses increase. Not even the most experienced school leader can know all that the future holds, but a good school leader must learn to think in such a way that he or she can better anticipate future events that could affect the school's financial situation.

To better anticipate events, a head of school can develop alternative budgets on the basis of futures research and past events and trends. These budgets would take into account possible changes in the community or school constituency that could affect expense or income assumptions. Then a school leader would need to ask these questions: If income unexpectedly decreases, how will we respond? If expenses unexpectedly increase, how will we respond? In other words, the head of school must be prepared to alter the budget in such a way that income and expenses remain balanced.

Leaders who make decisions ahead of time will have an easier time implementing those decisions in the heat of crisis, in part because people simply have greater confidence in leaders who make proactive decisions than in leaders who always seem to be reacting to the next crisis. Futures research is not difficult as long as you continually consider the following:

- *Need.* What need do you meet in your community? Do people in your community see you as meeting their needs? How do you know?
- *Target audience.* What does this population look like now? What trends are occurring? You must develop accurate information regarding its size, location, understanding of its need you can meet, and its understanding that you are the best option to meet that self-identified need.
- *Location and geography.* What travel habits does your core audience have? Are there any boundaries that people typically will not cross? What do you know of plans for housing or retail development in your area?

- *Competition.* Who else does what you do in your area? What common competitive factors will your core audience use to judge you and your competition? Are there any potential collaborators?
- *Funding.* What percentage of your current income comes from tuition? from fund-raising? Are you comfortable with those percentages? If not, what must you do to create a better balance?
- *Staffing.* Who will work for you in the future? Where will you find quality people who share your passion? What will it cost you to staff your school in three years? in five years? in ten years?
- *Assets.* What conclusions do you draw from considering the following assets: staff, facilities, land, location, brand reputation, and partnerships with churches or donors?
- *Social and lifestyle factors.* Who are the ones most likely to oppose your mission? What can you do to lessen their impact? Who are your natural allies in fulfilling your mission? How can you strengthen those partnerships? What trends will probably affect your ability to deliver your mission?
- *Political realities.* Who are your friends or foes at the local level: county and city government? zoning department? inspectors? Do any local or national laws concern you? How do you stay in touch with political developments?
- *Technological innovation.* What impact is technology likely to have on your instructional strategies, curriculum design, parent expectations, staff development, and competitive status and strategy?

Another important leadership element is at work here. The head of school who asks the board to solve a difficult problem has abdicated his or her leadership role. People easily lose faith in a leader who doesn't step up in a challenging situation. Once a person surrenders leadership, that person will find it nearly impossible to regain it. A person may remain in a leadership role, but people will afterward seldom view him or her as a leader. The damage to the leader's credibility is just too great. A leader must, as one of his or her primary jobs, anticipate and (when able) avoid problems. On those occasions when a school faces an unavoidable problem, the head of school must accept responsibility for both the problem and for an appropriate and timely solution.

Don't Forget the 2,000-Pound Elephant in the Back of the Room

Seldom does the leadership of a church-sponsored school ever build, approve, and implement a budget without significant influence by the senior pastor, the church's ruling board, or both. That reality can and often does cause significant conflict between a church and a school. I know of many quality school leaders who have left church-sponsored schools because of inability to resolve the tension between school and church leadership.

In my opinion the conflict over financial issues between a church and a school does not need to occur. It also presents a terrible testimony to a community and can have a negative impact on enrollment.

An Assumption and Two Recommendations

Assumption

Any church that chooses to sponsor a school has assumed a funding responsibility. The church must count the cost. Schooling is expensive in terms of both staffing and facilities. Run several hundred kids through a building daily and things will break, debris and dirt will accumulate, and wear and tear will require repair and replacement. In addition, the church and the school will probably compete for limited space, and someone will probably need to rearrange the rooms every weekend.

No church, therefore, should enter into such a relationship lightly. A church must take great care to ensure that the congregation and church leadership clearly understand that a schooling component is central to the church's mission and vision. Only when a church has established a fully shared mission will its leadership and congregation willingly bear the financial responsibility that comes with operating a school.

Many churches successfully and enthusiastically sponsor and provide strong financial support for a school. My granddaughters attended a Lutheran school for many years. The seamless, mutually beneficial relationship was a wonder to behold. The church facilities had been constructed with a school in mind. Both the pastor and the lay leadership fully supported the school. And my granddaughters benefited from a quality education offered at a reasonable price.

Recommendation 1

A church-sponsored school should create a separate budget that is completely distinct from the church budget, even if the church and the school operate under one nonprofit charter. An impermeable wall must separate the school's budget from the church's budget. Fund transfers may take place, but the budgets must remain independent of each other.

The financial resources necessary to fund the mission of a particular local church come primarily from the free-will giving of its members. The members of a local congregation give in response to their stewardship obligation and the church's specific needs. Following its specific governing principles, a local church then makes decisions about how best to use those financial resources to fulfill its mission.

Income in a school, on the other hand, comes primarily from tuition. A clear, even legal, agreement exists between a school and the parents who enroll their children in that school; parents pay tuition in exchange for educational and related services. This agreement exists whether a parent association owns the school or a church sponsors it. If a church used tuition revenue to fund church ministries rather than educational obligations, the church would be committing a serious ethical violation. And the same type of serious ethical violation occurs when money donated to the church goes toward supporting school operations. Without separate budgets, money too easily moves inappropriately from one organization to the other. The lines must be absolutely and unmistakably clear.

Recommendation 2

All transfers of funding from church to school or school to church should be clearly articulated in writing, and both governing bodies must authorize those transfers. When a church sponsors a school, the church can approach the funding obligations that come with that sponsorship in a number of ways.

It can, for example, decide to cover all costs related to the construction of the buildings, or it can lease space at a discounted rate. It can cover all costs related to maintenance and upkeep, or it can charge for a portion of those costs or for specific elements such as the salary of a janitor or the funding for a particular repair project. It can cover all costs related to utilities or charge the school for a particular percentage of those costs.

A church and a school can exercise complete flexibility in how they share those costs. They can exercise no flexibility, however, regarding how they build those costs into their budgets. For example, a church might decide to charge the school a rental fee for the use of church facilities. The school would build that rental cost into its budget and would then transfer funds to the church at appropriate times according to some kind of payment schedule.

I also believe that some kind of objective standard must guide any transfer of payment. For example, if the church decides to require a rental payment for the use of facilities, the church should investigate current rental rates in the local community and charge a fee that is based on those rates. By the same principle the church should set neither utility charges nor maintenance charges in an arbitrary fashion.

In a perfect world a sponsoring church would willingly cover costs related to the actual construction of the building. However, I believe a school should fully share the costs associated with occupying and operating a facility. In so doing, the school is accomplishing two important things.

First, an appropriate sharing of costs helps keep criticism of the school at a minimum. Members of the church who do not enroll students in the school often see the downside a lot more than they see the long-term impact in the lives of kids. The former perspective can lead to a bit of grumbling. In one way we can understand that perspective. Buildings do take a beating when a school occupies them. Taking responsibility for such facility abrasion sends a signal to the church that the school understands that reality and sees itself as a fully committed partner. Second, charging an appropriate amount for the care of facilities sends an appropriate signal to parents. They need to understand that the true cost of operating a school includes funding for facilities.

Conclusion

Building a budget has many dimensions. Among many others, organizational structure will influence both construction and oversight. As in any other organizational arena, schools must ensure clarity. All the appropriate parties must know, understand, and follow the rules. Where ambiguity exists, misunderstanding and conflict will follow. Don't ever allow either poor structure or poor practice to undermine your credibility as a leader or damage the reputation of your school. If you do, you'll find building a sustainable school difficult if not impossible.

Chapter Eight
Connecting Strategic Vision to Operational Reality

Sadly, few schools do strategic planning well, if at all. Indeed, most schools seem to exist in a state of perpetual crisis, lurching from one year to the next much like the nation of Israel wandering about the wilderness—forty years of discomfort and frustration and then eventually death—and all because of a bad decision based on fear and disbelief. Please don't let that trap catch you. Don't let the fear of the moment drive you. If God has a *purpose* for you and your school, He also has a *plan* for you and your school.

And remember this: strategic planning is not so much a development process as it is a discovery process. But when you are going through the discovery process, you are going through only one part of the process because, as Steven Case (former CEO of AOL) reminds us, "A vision without the ability to execute is a hallucination" (Kopelman 2006). Once we have clarity regarding how we can better become what God has called us to be, we must then develop a funding strategy that doesn't ignore either present reality or future needs. I'd like us to consider how schools develop that kind of funding strategy as part of a strategic-budgeting process.

The Strategic Connection

Let's begin this discussion by asking the following question: What happens when a school's yearly budgeting process and the periodic strategic-planning efforts of that school are disconnected? I'll tell you what I've discovered in most schools. Only you can decide whether the school you lead suffers from these consequences.

Consequence 1: Difficult, Ongoing Debates over Tuition Rates

I want to focus on a question I believe skews the entire budgeting process while preventing the kinds of strategic decisions necessary for building a strong school and a stable future. You know the question. You may have even asked this question at one time or another. It goes something like this: "So how much of an increase in the tuition rate can our parents handle this year?"

Not only do you know the question, but you know the standard reply as well: "Not very much." So on the basis of nothing more than the barest of anecdotal evidence and everyone's fears and assumptions, your tuition rate is set at some artificial figure with no real thought regarding how that figure will affect your ability to address important tactical issues and strategic initiatives.

Consequence 2: Short-Circuited Discussion of Faculty and Staff Compensation

In all the strategic-planning processes I've led, every school listed the need to increase faculty and staff compensation as a priority. And yet in all these years, I can recall only one time when a school adopted and then implemented a compensation initiative. Everyone knows that insufficient compensation is a problem—a problem that, by the way, is only going to worsen. But the following question, answer, and action hijack every attempt to address a legitimate concern:

- *Question:* "How much more do the faculty and staff need?"
- *Answer:* "More than we can give them."
- *Action:* The debate ends, though with heavy hearts.

We know that it is a problem, perhaps even a life-threatening problem, but we feel helpless to do anything significant. So we continue to lose great teachers, especially men, who simply can't afford to support their passion. They resign. They feel guilty. We feel defeated. And all these negative results occur because we can't figure out a way to strategically and realistically address the compensation issue.

Consequence 3: Wishful Projections for Enrollment

Need more money in your budget? Schools all over the country employ a simple solution. Just pretend that the extra twenty students you need to balance your budget will show up. It's a corollary to the "build it and they will come" fantasy. Believe me when I say that serious consequences always result when projected enrollment figures don't materialize as expected. More space won't automatically produce more growth, nor will your budget needs magically produce additional students. You have to do the hard work of customer service, excellent instruction, and effective marketing to ensure adequate numbers of new and returning students.

Costs seldom decline. So imagine what you create when you add a reluctance to charge a realistic tuition to cover constantly increasing costs. That's right; you create enrollment inflation. And nothing will put you at greater financial risk. Yet schools find few beliefs more seductive during the budgeting process.

Consequence 4: Growing Dependence on Annual-Funding Activities

In the early years of Christian schooling, we attempted to bridge the gap in our operational budgets through product sales of all kinds—from candy bars to citrus fruit to Christmas wrapping paper. Then along came the 'thons (jog, golf, walk, bowl), the festivals, and the auctions. Now more schools are engaging in annual-fund programs, which are a far better approach.

But even annual-fund strategies will struggle to succeed if a school is primarily trying to fund a gap in its operational budget. In addition, schools too easily inflate income projections from "fund-raising" activities. The reasoning goes like this. If we were able to raise $50,000 last year, then $60,000 or even $70,000 should be doable this year if we just work a little harder. And since we need an additional $20,000 to balance our projected budget, then why not?

Why not? Well, first of all, wishful thinking is not a strategy. Second, remember that the household income of your families and supporters is a variable. You can't control the level of discretionary income of your families. Nor can you guarantee that they will continue to support you as they have in the past. Third, remember that you will hit a ceiling regarding how much you can expect to raise through annual-fund efforts once they become mature and superb. Unless you can grow your support list at a healthy rate each year, you can't count on continuing increases in annual-fund income.

Consequence 5: Insufficient Funding for Reserve Funds and Facility Maintenance

When I mention reserve funds to the average Christian school leader, I often see a wry smile and a shrug of the shoulders. Board members give me a "you've got to be kidding; we can't even meet payroll" kind of look. Yet as I've already addressed, any school's financial health requires unrestricted funds for facility maintenance and crisis situations.

What amazes me is how often a school that contends it has no money to build into a reserve fund manages to find the money for the debt service required to repay a loan for replacing a roof on its gymnasium. Doesn't it make more sense to pay yourself than to pay the bank?

Consequence 6: Ignoring Long-Term Strategic Issues

The author of Proverbs makes an insightful observation when he writes, "Hope deferred makes the heart sick" (Proverbs 13:12). I find a lot of heart-sickness among Christian school leaders, teachers, parents, students, and board members. School leaders who are seeking to encourage a school constituency far too commonly make promises of better things tomorrow. Hope is a good thing, but hope is not a strategy. Unless leaders tie their promises to practical solutions, hope morphs into a toxin that tears at the soul of an organization.

Without a sound strategic-budgeting process, a school will find it difficult to develop workable solutions to perplexing problems, especially when those solutions come with a price tag. It doesn't take much effort to persuade people to identify real needs. Prioritizing those needs can be tricky, but it doesn't take long for people to agree on and commit to common goals when they have the right process in place. Funding those common goals, however, can present a real problem, especially when a leadership team will not change its funding paradigm or begin thinking in a time frame longer than a single year.

Does any of the above describe your budgeting realities? I suspect so, unless your school is among the small number that have already made a shift in how they view finance and budgeting. If any of the above does describe you, know this: there is hope. You will always face a challenge when budgeting, but you can begin changing your financial landscape if you will shift your thinking from a single-year to a long-term approach in budgeting—and if you have the wisdom and courage to face reality.

Done right, long-term budgeting (three to five years) created in concert with your strategic-planning process, will allow you to begin addressing seemingly resistant issues such as compensation for faculty and staff. It will also allow you—in fact, it will force you—to develop an effective communication strategy to keep your parents and supporters fully aware of your financial realities. You must take the essential first step of developing such a strategy if you want to build into your constituents the depth of understanding essential to effective annual-fund and capital-giving efforts.

A Strategic-Budgeting Illustration

In writing this chapter I benefited greatly from resources developed by Independent School Management (ISM) of Wilmington, Delaware. ISM provides helpful material on topics related to school finance, resource development, student recruitment, and retention.

The chart in figure 1 was modified from *Ideas and Perspectives* (ISM 1997).

Figure 1: Sample Strategic Financial Plan (SFP)
Dollar figures in thousands (000s)

	Year 1	Year 2	Year 3	Year 4	Year 5
1. Enrollment	200	200	200	200	200
2. Net tuition revenue	$1,000	$1,075	$1,156	$1,242	$1,335
3. Other hard income	50	50	50	50	50
4. Total hard income	$1,050	$1,125	$1,206	$1,292	$1,385
5. Operational expenses	$1,167	$1,214	$1,262	$1,313	$1,365
6. Hard income P & (L)	($117)	($89)	($56)	($21)	20
7. Hard income % coverage	90%	92.7%	95.6%	98.4%	101.5%
8. Annual (non-capital) fund-raising	$100	$100	$100	$100	$100
9. Overall P & (L)	($17)	$11	$44	$79	$120
10. Annual to reserve funds	$0	$11	$44	$79	$71
11. Total reserve funds	$0	$11	$55	$134	$205
12. Annual to endowment (by policy)	$0	$0	$0	$0	$49
13. Total endowment	$250	$250	$250	$250	$299

The SFP shown above assumes
- that the school's cash position and zero reserve funds require rapid strategic reversal;
- that the reversal can be accomplished without the marketing-and-enrollment risks inherent in cutting programs, services, or positions;
- that enrollment can be stabilized at current levels (N = 200);
- that expenses must be increased at inflation-plus-2.0%/year in order to move compensation and professional-growth funds forward in real (i.e., purchasing-power-adjusted) dollars; and
- that (net) tuition increases of inflation-plus-5.5%/year must therefore be accepted for the duration of the SFP.

Inflation is assumed at 2.0%/year.

What do you see? Carefully examine the above illustration and consider the following:
- Which numbers remain static from year to year?
- Which numbers change from year to year?
- How has revenue for funding operational costs and special costs shifted?

- Note the following assumptions:
  - Inflation is assumed at 2 percent per year.
  - Tuition must typically increase at the rate of inflation plus 2 to 3 percent simply to maintain operational programs at current levels.
  - Most schools offer tuition discounts of some kind; thus we speak of net tuition revenue rather than tuition revenue.
  - "Other hard income" assumes that the hard costs for providing the auxiliary programs have already been removed.
  - The further assumption is that all auxiliary programs will fully cover their hard costs and produce profit for the school.

By continuing to look at the strategic-budgeting illustration, let's begin to address the questions and assumptions I've just listed.

Which Numbers Remain Static from Year to Year?

Answers
- Enrollment
- Other hard income
- Annual (non-capital) fund-raising

As you may expect, you need to overcome some difficult obstacles when developing a budget extending beyond a single year. To reduce the number of obstacles and to inject a necessary dose of reality to the process, you must commit to resisting the impulse to build a budget on the basis of wishful thinking. Remember, unless you have unmistakable, compelling evidence to the contrary, you must always build a budget on your current enrollment numbers. Wishful thinking is OK in stories that begin with "once upon a time," but it has no place in budget development for a Christian school.

If you anticipate enrollment increases, along with artificially inflating annual-fund revenue projections, you are taking the easy way of dealing with constantly rising operational costs and funding for strategic initiatives. Avoid falling into that trap at all costs. Down that road lies financial ruin.

I do believe that schools can do more, much more, in developing strong streams of auxiliary revenue. In creating a long-term strategic budget, however, you cannot assume growth. You could choose to designate any revenue increases generated from auxiliary activities for program-enhancement projects or targeted scholarships. By doing so, you have increased the motivation to build better auxiliary programs without at the same time creating an operational dependence on those increases.

Which Numbers Change from Year to Year?

Answers

- Net tuition revenue
- Total hard income
- Operational expenses
- Hard income % coverage
- Annual-fund distribution

Can you remember a single year in which your operational costs declined rather than increased? Probably not, unless you experienced a significant decrease in enrollment or you eliminated entire programs. Costs nearly always go up, and in education the angle of ascent resembles the trajectory of the latest rocket launch at Cape Kennedy—straight up and accelerating.

So can we safely assume increased costs even with a static enrollment? The answer, of course, is yes. In fact, that assumption forms the basis for the strategic-budgeting illustration. When I hear of boards or administrators who issue a directive to hold the line on tuition increases, I know I'm hearing about a school on a collision course with reality. And in that contest reality always wins.

If nothing changes at your school—no new faculty or staff hires, no new programs, no new facilities, no changes in debt service—you must count on increasing your tuition rate by the rate of inflation plus 2 to 3 percent just to stay even from year to year. For example, if your tuition income for the previous year was $5,000 and inflation is projected at 3 percent during the year, then you would need to increase your tuition rate to between $5,250 and $5,300 just to stay level with the current year. So your tuition would need to increase to about $6,600 over a five-year span just to maintain current programmatic and compensation levels.

Now imagine the impact on tuition rates if you seriously desire to address faculty and staff compensation. You simply cannot solve long-term issues such as low faculty and staff compensation or a built-in gap for funding operational costs unless you are willing to deal with the problems created by keeping your tuition artificially low. Your goal must be 100 percent funding of operations from operational revenue.

What-If Scenario Planning and Your Strategic Budget

Once you have made a strategic decision to increase faculty and staff salaries to 80 percent of the salaries at local public schools, for example, scenario planning allows you to consider how your strategic decision will affect your budget over the next five years.

In a scenario-planning process, there are no right and wrong answers. You simply introduce certain variables and then consider their impact. At any point you can change the variables, but at all times you keep the same goal. You want to discover the real costs inherent in achieving a particular strategic goal over a five-year span. With those numbers in mind, you must then decide to proceed or consider altering your goal.

At this point many schools turn back. The numbers scare them. I understand that response. It is good to take a long, hard look at reality before plunging ahead with any plan. If, however, the goal is truly strategic, if it will help elevate your school to a higher level of excellence, then you will be doing the right thing by moving ahead even if you find the numbers a bit daunting.

You can approach this process in several different ways. You can look at salaries for all faculty and staff, for just full-time faculty and staff, for just staff, for just faculty, or any other combination. As you run those various scenarios, you will benefit from asking the following questions:
- Can we eliminate any current positions?
- How will we cover the responsibilities of any eliminated positions? Are those suggestions realistic, or will we diminish our ability to perform well in crucial areas?

- Can we reduce staff by increasing efficiency?
  - Are current staff operating at peak performance?
  - Why or why not?
  - Is it a morale problem, a resource problem, a knowledge problem, a skill problem, a talent problem, or some combination of those?
- Can we eliminate any of our current programs? How will doing so affect staffing needs?
- Do we need to add any programs? How will doing so affect staffing needs?

Part of any scenario-planning process that looks at faculty and staff salaries requires a comprehensive evaluation of current and future staffing needs. This is a time for absolute honesty. If everyone is struggling just to keep his or her head above water, you are pretending if you think you can benefit from eliminating staff as a way to decrease costs or to increase staff compensation. But if you are simply protecting someone out of a sense of loyalty, now is the time to make a change.

This is also the time for a little creative thinking as well as the time to challenge certain professional paradigms that may significantly affect staffing decisions. For example, in most schools the responsibility of teacher supervision falls on a principal or a head of school. Why? Why not assign new teachers to an experienced master teacher who will serve in the role of mentor? When classroom observation makes sense, hire a substitute teacher for a day to cover the mentor's classes. Who is better able to evaluate a teacher's performance than an exceptional teacher? As another example, wouldn't it make more sense to hire a staff assistant who has the right gifts to address any administrative needs rather than to remove a quality teacher from the classroom and force that teacher into an administrative role?

You must ask those kinds of questions during a scenario-planning process. Running numbers is crucial but insufficient. You must ask and answer this question first: To fulfill our mission with excellence, how must we staff ourselves? Then you must determine the true cost of doing so in a manner that respects pertinent biblical principles while allowing you to attract and retain the best people available.

During a recent strategic-planning process, the leadership of one school I was working with decidedn to address the problem of inadequate faculty compensation. The leadership set the goal of increasing all faculty and staff salaries to 80 percent of the salaries at local public schools. The school leadership took on the task of scenario planning, that is, of demonstrating the budget impact of achieving the 80-percent goal. The chart in figure 2 (following the six questions) provides an overall answer to that question. To create the chart, the leadership sought answers to the following questions.

Question 1. What is the current staff configuration?
- What is the current number of
  - faculty?
  - instructional support staff?
  - administrative support staff?
  - auxiliary staff?
- For faculty and staff, what are the current
  - academic qualifications?
  - field-experience qualifications?

Question 2. What is the current staff compensation structure? You need this information to develop a baseline from which to structure a five-year implementation plan. In this case the leadership determined the average current faculty and staff salaries to be about 60 percent of comparable salaries at local public schools.

Question 3. Should we reconfigure our current staff on the basis of strategic initiatives and scenario research? If so, how will doing so affect the number and responsibilities of
- faculty?
- instructional support staff?
- administrative support staff?
- auxiliary staff?

Question 4. What salary goals do we want to achieve over the next five years?
- Changes in base salaries?
- Changes in salary adjustments related to
  - degree level?
  - experience?
  - stipends for additional responsibility?

Question 5. What is the yearly financial impact if we are going to accomplish our 80-percent goal?

Question 6. Is this a realistic goal for our school to pursue?
- Is this the right strategic goal?
- Is it reasonable?
  - Can we meet all our other goals and keep the percentage of our budget dedicated to compensation at 70 percent or less?
  - Can we make a case to our parents and supporters that maintaining and improving our ability to deliver our mission with excellence requires that we meet this goal?

	Year 1	Year 2	Year 3	Year 4	Year 5
Figure 2: Illustration of Increasing Faculty Salaries					
Goal: To increase faculty salaries from 60% of public school faculty salaries to 80% of public school faculty salaries over five years.					
Average public school faculty salaries	$50,000	$51,500	$53,045	$54,636	$56,275
Average Christian school faculty salaries	$30,000	$33,475	$37,131	$40,975	$45,020
Total for 20 public school teachers	$1,000,000	$1,030,000	$1,060,900	$1,092,727	$1,125,509
Total for 20 Christian school teachers	$600,000	$669,500	$742,630	$819,545	$900,410

Notes

1. To achieve the goal of increasing from 60% to 80% of local public school salaries, teachers would require an increase of 50% in salaries.
2. This is based on the premise that public school teacher salaries would increase on average 3% per year.
3. Assuming an enrollment of 400, the increase in tuition to cover increases in teacher salaries would be $750 per student over five years.
4. This illustration assumes no increase in enrollment or in the number of full-time faculty positions.
5. Assuming a tuition rate of $6,500, that would mean a tuition increase of 12% over five years.
6. This illustration does not reflect increases in salaries for administrators, support staff, part-time faculty, or coaching supplements.
7. This illustration does not reflect increases in operating costs during the same period.
8. Typically tuition must increase by the rate of inflation plus 3% every year to maintain current programs.
9. The primary purpose of this exercise is to show how significant changes can be made when planning occurs over a five-year period rather than trying to adjust from year to year.

Schools should use similar scenario-planning processes to address any number of issues that will affect the budgeting process. Through sound scenario-planning processes, schools can best answer questions ranging from facility needs to new-program development to resource-development strategies.

If you don't feel equipped to lead these kinds of activities or if you value the objectivity of a fresh set of eyes, seek outside counsel.

I recognize that you will need to make a considerable investment of time to gather and consider all this information. You must make that investment, however, if your school's leadership team expects to meet its obligations well. Unless you can develop a transitional plan that allows you to consider cost impact, you will probably never take on the kinds of challenges you must face to create a school of excellence.

Conclusion

You don't need to create a five-year strategic budget every year, though I think it is a good exercise. Whenever you engage in a strategic-planning process, however, you must include a strategic-budgeting activity. Any strategic initiatives you identify will probably remain unfunded or underfunded unless you do.

In addition, strategic budgeting allows you to communicate to your entire constituency that the school leadership team is thinking and acting wisely— in other words, that the team is counting the cost. You will build greater support for your efforts from parents, current donors, and potential donors. It is one thing to discover and communicate a vision. It is quite another to fund that vision. The right kind of strategic budgeting will increase the probability that your vision will become reality.

Chapter Nine
The Essential First Step to Building the Budget

My goal in this chapter is to give you a better understanding of the nuts-and-bolts process for developing your expense assumptions. In building a budget, a school's leadership must begin by determining as accurately as possible the expenses for operating the school in the coming year. To do that appropriately, a school leadership team must first understand the concept of a *cost center* in the same way a for-profit business does.

Cost Centers

A cost center is a "distinctly identifiable department, division, or unit of a firm whose managers are responsible for all associated costs and for ensuring adherence to its cost budgets" (businessdictionary.com). Unfortunately, schools do not create budgets that show costs distinctly identifiable with a particular department. Nor do schools typically hold anyone other than the head of school responsible for income or costs associated with those departments. Schools need to stop making those mistakes.

Now let me break that information down a bit and apply it directly to your school situation. Too often schools cannot determine the true costs of providing a particular service or addressing a specific need. In the typical school budget, for example, the leadership team places all compensation costs for all the school's employees in a single budget item labeled "faculty and staff salaries" or something similar. This approach hides the real cost of operating such programs as athletics or resource development.

For example, in most school budgets, series of line items detail income from resource-development activities such as a golf marathon, an annual-fund banquet, or an auction. Those line items typically, however, show only the hard costs for a particular event. Budgets seldom consider staffing and infrastructure costs. Thus schools have an incomplete understanding of the true cost of events and thus the true net revenue resulting from the events.

Consider this simple illustration. Let's say that your school sponsors a yearly auction that generates $40,000 of gross revenue. Your hard costs for such an event may come from items such as decorations, food, printing, and advertising—all totaling $7,000. Most of the time a school would then declare the event a success because it had generated a $33,000 profit.

What would occur, however, if the school was to consider all the costs associated with the event? Let's say, for example, that your director of development has invested a third of her time for the year in planning and leading this event. And let's say that the total compensation for that person is $36,000 a year. You need to subtract that $12,000 cost from the total, reducing your profit to $21,000. All of a sudden your margin on the event is not looking as good, and you have not finished yet. Now you must consider all the other infrastructure costs from planning and producing the event. Did other staff help? What about use of the office copier? What about utility costs or setup and cleaning costs if the event took place on campus? Added together, those expenses may easily add another $2,000 or $3,000 to the costs of the event. Once again your profit line takes a hit.

Consider a second illustration. What does it take to operate your interscholastic athletic program? As long as you lump all your compensation and infrastructure costs into other categories, you'll never know. Do you have any teachers who also function as coaches? If so, do you show that cost as part of your athletic program? Probably not.

Do your coaches make use of your copy machines? Probably. Where do you show the cost of those copies? Unless you charge those various costs to the athletic department, you can't show the real cost of your athletic program. But you might ask, Does that matter? And that would be a fair question. Here's the answer. You simply can't make wise decisions without accurate information.

Since athletics can be a significant cost center in any school, let's dig a little deeper. School leaders will often say to me, "Dr. Pue, we just can't attract enough students to our school without a strong and varied athletic program." Here is my response. Perhaps that is true, but what evidence do you track that allows you to make that case? Can you demonstrate that your athletic program actually produces additional students, support, and income? If you can't, then your first action should be to find a way to collect that information, which would serve as the evidence you need when making a cost-benefit analysis. In doing so, you are simply weighing all the costs over time against expected benefits over time to answer this question: Do the benefits outweigh the costs?

Now, the benefits do not always come in the form of dollars and cents. Sometimes the benefits come in the form of school reputation, public relations opportunities, or the mentoring opportunities that come with quality coaches who intensely interact with student athletes. Although you will have difficulty quantifying those kinds of benefits, you should be able to track students who enroll at your school directly because of any quality program.

You can look at program decisions another way. Suppose you decide to invest resources in your science and math programs rather than in your athletic programs. In part you may base the decision on a particular philosophy. You may also base the decision on a more pragmatic foundation. Perhaps no local school has a reputation for a quality science or math program or technological program or fine arts program or cross-cultural program or any number of other imaginative offerings.

As I mentioned, a well-developed mission analysis as well as a sound cost-benefit analysis should determine those kinds of decisions. I have found, however, that neither a mission analysis nor a cost-benefit analysis drives those kinds of decisions. They tend, instead, to have as their driving force the desires of a particular person or of a group of people or the less-than-compelling argument, "That's just what you do in high school." May I suggest that "all schools have athletic programs" (or fine arts programs or whatever) does not translate into a sound argument regarding either mission development or budget development in a Christian school.

The Ultimate Rationale

You may be saying, "OK, you've convinced me that cost-center budgeting and cost-benefit analyses make great sense. But I have two final questions. Why develop expense assumptions first? Shouldn't we figure out how much money we have to work with before going to all the trouble of creating a budget?"

These questions are important. The answer is simple. Every head of school bears the responsibility for determining the cost of providing an education that fully achieves the school's mission with excellence and integrity. To do otherwise is to dishonor God and disregard the promises the school has made to its parents, students, teachers, and community.

When the budgeting process begins with income assumptions, a school will find it too easy to shape its program on the basis of those assumptions rather than on the school's stated mission, core values, and desired outcomes. Certainly financial realities sometimes require a school leader to adjust priorities and goals. When those adjustments turn into an ongoing reality, however, the school leadership needs to reexamine self-defined core issues related to both purpose and practice.

School boards that insist on building a budget beginning with income assumptions rather than expense assumptions often find their school stuck in a perpetual state of inertia, their head of school and his or her staff frustrated, and their parents on the hunt for something better. Why? Because when you begin with income, you never seem to have enough money to do what is truly remarkable—what can help elevate the school to greater levels of excellence.

Anytime you want to lock up the imagination in an organization, simply say the following: "There isn't enough money to do that." Unfortunately, school boards commonly make that comment when they begin the budgeting process with income assumptions. Keep saying, "Nice idea, but there just isn't enough money this year," and you'll probably never find the money to fund the really transforming idea that could change everything at your school; and worse, you'll probably lose the person who keeps bringing those brilliant but annoyingly expensive ideas to your attention.

Although the approach I am recommending may appear a bit more cumbersome, you will not find it difficult to maintain once you have it in place, and it is the only way to provide accurate income and expense assumptions for all you do as a school. To develop a sense for how I recommend you structure your budget, look at the following categories, noting how I have broken down the budget into distinct cost-center categories.

Recommended Cost Centers for Developing a School Budget

- Instructional Costs
  - Preschool
  - Elementary
  - Middle school
  - High school
- Administrative and support expenses
- Cocurricular programs
  - Athletics
  - Fine arts
  - Other
- Advancement expenses
  - Resource development
  - Student recruitment and retention
  - Public relations
- Plant operations
  - Maintenance
  - Landscaping
  - Utilities
  - Rent/lease/debt service
  - Projects
- Institutionally funded financial aid
- Auxiliary-services expenses (the number of these services will vary from school to school, but here are some examples)
  - Food service
  - Before- and after-school care
  - Summer programs
  - Transportation service

The following is a sample cost-center budget for instructional costs.

Figure 3: Illustration of a Sample Cost-Center Budget Cost center: Instructional costs/Total	
Preschool costs	$353,532
Elementary costs	$283,960
Middle school costs	$228,240
High school costs	$289,520
Online costs	
Total instructional costs	$1,155,252

Notes
1. These numbers are used only as an illustration. They are not based on research, nor are they intended to be used as recommended numbers.
2. Based on the following enrollments:
   - Preschool: 102 @ $3,466/student
   - Elementary: 124 @ $2,290/student
   - Middle school: 72 @ $3,170/student
   - High school: 88 @ $3,290/student
   - Total: 386 @ $3,330/student
3. Based on the following number of instructional personnel:
   - Preschool: FT, 6; PT, 6
   - Elementary: FT, 5; PT, 3
   - Middle school: FT, 4; PT, 3
   - High school: FT, 5; PT, 3
   - Total: FT, 20; PT, 15
4. Based on an average FT salary of $30,000
5. Remember that the staffing numbers do not include any administrative, support, athletic, advancement, or plant operation personnel. This includes only instructional personnel.
6. You should develop a similar cost-center budget for each of your cost centers.

To ensure accurate cost analysis you must insist that each cost center use the same set of categories and subcategories even though a particular category or subcategory may not apply to the cost center. In so doing, you are using the best way to show true costs for each category. See figure 4.

Figure 4: Illustration of Sample Categories for Cost-Center Budget Cost center: Instructional costs, high school	
Categories	
1. Compensation	$257,355
2. Professional development	$6,000
3. Curriculum	$12,000
4. Telecommunications	$600
5. Library	$3,000
6. Equipment	$5,000
7. Furniture	$1,200
8. Supplies	$3,000
9. Printing	$600
10. Copies	$2,000
11. Events	$600
12. Transportation	
13. Travel	$1,200
14. Marketing	
15. Other	$600
Total costs	$293,155

Notes:
1. Based on an enrollment of 88.
2. Based on 5 FT and 3 PT faculty and 25 days of substitutes.
3. Based on an average FT salary of $30,000, PT salary of $18,000.
4. These numbers may vary significantly from one school to the next. They serve only to illustrate how to create a cost-centered budget.
5. You can create as much detail in this portion of the budget as you desire, showing every subcategory under each of the main categories. A list of all main categories with their subcategories can be found below.
6. For example, you could show the following subcategories under the category of compensation:
   a. Salary
   b. Social Security
   c. Retirement
   d. Health insurance
   e. Other

Recommended Subcategories for Each Cost-Center Category

- Compensation
  - Salary
  - Social Security
  - Retirement
  - Health insurance
  - Other
- Professional development
  - Continuing education
  - Workshops/seminars
  - Conferences
  - Other
- Telecommunications
  - Phone/cell service
  - Internet service
  - Other
- Curriculum
  - Textbooks
  - Software
  - Teaching aids
  - Other
- Library/research
  - Books
  - Software
  - Internet service
  - Supplies
  - Equipment
  - Furniture
  - Other
- Equipment
  - Purchase
  - Repair
  - Other

- Furniture
  - Purchase
  - Repair
  - Other
- Supplies
  - Paper
  - Office supplies
  - Cleaning supplies
  - Athletic supplies
  - Classroom supplies
  - Lab supplies
  - Other
- Printing
  - Stationery
  - Communications
  - Other
- Copier
  - Purchase
  - Lease
  - Repair/maintenance
  - Supplies
- Events
  - Marketing
  - Materials
  - Rental
  - Facilities use
  - Food Other
- Transportation
  - Purchase
  - Lease
  - Repair
  - Fuel
  - Other

- Travel
  - Airfare
  - Rental car
  - Mileage
  - Fuel
  - Hotel
  - Parking
  - Meals
  - Other
- Marketing
  - Advertising
  - Website development/maintenance
  - Postage
  - Design
  - Other
- Other

When the cost-center documents are completed, you will have three levels of budget reports. The micro level will contain all the financial data for each subcategory. For example, under the cost center Instructional Costs you will show all relevant costs for Preschool, Elementary, Middle School, and High School.

You will then collapse all that data to show total expenses under the cost center Instructional Costs. Then you will collapse all the cost-center data into one final budget showing the combined costs from all your cost centers in a single document. This will be the public document you might distribute to your parents.

In other words you will have three sets of budget documents, moving from the greatest level of detail to a summary of all costs. Developing your budget in this manner allows you to determine true costs while providing a usable summary budget for public discussion. You can explode or collapse your budget to expose as much or as little detail as you desire for a particular conversation or discussion.

You may want to change some of my categories, but I recommend that you maintain the approach. In no other way can you determine the true costs of operating a particular program at your school.

Your Biggest and Most Important Investment

However you choose to structure your budget, you will face one constant. By far the largest percentage of your budget will go toward personnel— somewhere between 70 and 80 percent in the typical school. If you are going to spend that kind of money, doesn't it make sense to invest it wisely? Here are some thoughts I hope will help you do just that.

Determining Legitimate Staffing Needs

Various considerations will influence decisions about staffing needs. First, you need to consider the size of your school. Second, you need to consider the nature of your program. For example, a comprehensive upper-school program would entail significantly greater faculty and staffing needs than would a small K–6 school consisting of a single section in each grade. Schools often put themselves at financial risk because they staff inappropriately for their size or because they do not set tuition levels correctly.

You can offer any kind of program you desire if you will charge an appropriate tuition. If, however, you insist on artificially depressing your tuition to satisfy a desire to keep tuition "affordable," you will probably experience continuing financial challenges.

Schools also often make the mistake of failing to connect the right person— meaning the person possessing the right combination of character, talent, knowledge, experience, and skill—to the right job, meaning a specific, well-defined role that when done with excellence creates the best-possible outcome for the school.

To support the instructional mission of your school, you should obviously set the goal of hiring the best teachers possible. We tend, however, to hire the best teachers possible who are willing or able to work for the wages we offer them. Mediocre and poor teachers, however, come with a hidden cost: poor retention.

Schools must hire the best—not only for teaching positions, but for administrative and support positions as well. Here schools face even greater challenges because of the difficulty of developing quality job descriptions for leadership and support positions. I encourage school leaders and school boards to educate themselves on how to define leadership and support roles in an environment in which technology is rapidly changing nearly every job in every sector of society.

I tend to believe that schools should keep their administrative support staff to a minimum. I suspect that some reading those words would disagree. They might look at themselves or at the staff they lead and see people whose work schedules look somewhat like my plate at Thanksgiving: full to over-flowing. Those people would look at me and say, "Dr. Pue, we need more staff members, not fewer. My staff members have more to do than anyone should be asked to do. I can't believe you would recommend fewer staff." I appreciate those concerns but I'd ask you to consider the following.

Don't just add support staff because someone feels overwhelmed. First find out why that person feels overwhelmed. The position may require more than is humanly possible. The position, however, may entail too many different kinds of jobs, each requiring different talents and skills. School leaders often subscribe to the motto "If you need a job done, find a busy person and give it to that person."

Subscribing to that motto is a bad idea. Instead, find a specific person who has the right kind of talent and the appropriate skills and then hire that person for a clearly defined job to which those specific talents and skills will directly apply. In fact, I would rather hire several part-time staff whose talents and skills clearly connect to their specific tasks than have a single, dedicated-but-overwhelmed "jack of all trades and master of none" doing a job that the school has cobbled together much like Frankenstein's monster.

I promise you that the return on investment will be much higher if you do what I have recommended. You will have more-motivated, more-productive employees and as a result more-confident, more-content customers. Both are necessary and good for the school's financial stability. Make a wrong call on either the person or the job description, however, and you have taken the first step toward staff frustration and mediocre performance. Hire the right people, compensate them appropriately, give them clear mandates, lead them wisely, provide them with the necessary resources, and you will reap enormous benefits.

A school, regardless of its size, makes its most important staffing decision, of course, when it calls a head of school. In one sense the rules that apply to choosing faculty and support staff also apply to choosing the head of school. You have to find the right combination of character, talent, knowledge, experience, and skill—all in someone who shares a passion for your purpose. In addition, your head of school must possess a thorough understanding of and appreciation for the distinct culture of your school and community, and he or she needs to have demonstrated the capacity for the kind of leadership any organization requires to move into the future with confidence, creativity, and excellence.

Schools face a tough task here, one we make harder because often we refuse to compensate the right person appropriately and because we are confused about how best to define the role of head of school in our current era. Too often we are looking for someone like Mr. Chips, that kindly academic who so loves kids that he is willing to make any sacrifice to touch their lives.

I think it is good to find passionate people who will sacrifice in pursuit of a great mission. But I think it is equally good to find remarkable people who then perform jobs for which God has clearly gifted them. Failure to connect talent to task, especially when choosing a head of school, will inevitably lead to frustration and failure. That failure may also help explain the kind of unhealthy turnover rates we see in Christian school leadership.

Determining Staff Compensation

When you determine compensation, you are making decisions about far more than salary alone. However, I want to begin our conversation with the question of how much you should pay your staff. I will confess that I have strong beliefs on this matter. I began my teaching career at a Christian school, and I can still remember the days when I had no idea how I would provide for my family. The school where I taught paid ridiculously low salaries. My wife and I faced a continuing challenge just finding ways to make it through the month. You are, of course, familiar with that reality.

At the beginning of this discussion, I believe it is crucial to understand that Scripture does not support the substandard salaries that so many Christian schools offer. The Scriptures clearly teach that "the laborer is worthy of his wages" (1 Timothy 5:18, NASB). That is not a difficult verse to understand. It simply means that you are supposed to pay a worker according to how the culture at large values his or her specific work. Even though you may find it difficult to compensate your teachers in the same manner as local public schools compensate their teachers, I think you must acknowledge that competent, qualified teachers who invest in the lives of students should receive remuneration at as high a level as possible. Every school should make doing so a priority.

Even if we set aside the Scripture for a second, it simply makes sense to provide good compensation to your staff. Adequate salaries help you recruit and retain exceptional teachers, without whom you cannot deliver a quality program. I will go so far as saying that quality teachers can make a huge difference in your reenrollment percentages. Parents will be far more reluctant to withdraw their students from a school where the teachers are simply the best. Imagine the financial impact if your retention numbers increase from the typical 75 to 80 percent to 90 to 95 percent!

You will always, of course, experience a tension between paying the highest possible salaries and keeping tuition at reasonable levels. Christian teachers should not, however, bear the brunt of the sacrifice. Parents and teachers must share any necessary sacrifice in an equitable way.

Developing a salary schedule

Any salary schedule should, at minimum, take into account two key elements: educational level and years of experience. In addition, a school should always build in some supplementary compensation for any added responsibility related directly to instructional activity. For example, a school should provide an additional stipend to a teacher for acting as a head teacher, a department head, or a mentor for new teachers. The same principle applies for those who serve as coaches of sports teams or those who provide leadership for other school-sponsored programs beyond the classroom.

Further, I think it wise to consider building in some kind of bonus for teachers and staff who perform at exceptional levels. I know that merit pay is a hot-button issue in education. Often people raise the question, How do you decide which performance determines which teacher is superior? They are asking a fair question, but it does not change the reality. We all know that some teachers simply do a better job. And you can find ways to judge performance quality, from peer and student reviews to evaluation of test results to personal observation. Typically schools do not have the problem of finding a *way* to evaluate performance as much as they have the problem of finding the *will* to evaluate performance.

Many for-profit companies evaluate performance by creating a framework for evaluating performance and then using the flexibility of a salary band at each level of education and experience to offer some additional compensation. Take a look at the Sample Salary Schedule table in figure 5. Remember this: what you don't reward disappears. I think you will be acting both wisely and biblically if you reward quality performance.

We must address one additional salary issue: How do we compensate key administrative staff, including the head of school? Most administrative staff members are twelve-month employees, and most bear greater responsibility for the health of the school than do most teachers. For those reasons alone they should receive a greater level of compensation than teachers. Since the head of school bears the greatest responsibility, he or she should receive the highest level of compensation.

Schools face even greater difficulty finding quality leaders than they do finding quality teachers. Poor compensation compounds the problem in part because the scarcity of good candidates may cause schools to face fierce competition when trying to hire a good candidate.

Here is a rule of thumb for deciding the compensation for your head of school. Determine how much you would compensate the person if he or she served as a teacher in your school. Let's say that the person has fifteen years' experience and a master's degree. On the salary schedule illustration in fugure 5, those qualifications would mean a salary of $41,250.

Figure 5: Sample Salary Schedule
(These numbers are for illustration only; they are not intended as recommendations.)

Experi-ence (years)	BA	BA+9	BA+18	BA+27	MA/ MEd	MA/ MEd +24	PhD/ EdD
0	$27,000	$27,500	$28,000	$28,500	$30,000	$30,500	$32,000
1	$27,500	$28,000	$28,500	$29,000	$30,500	$31,000	$32,500
2	$28,000	$28,500	$29,000	$29,500	$31,000	$31,500	$33,000
3	$28,500	$29,000	$29,500	$30,000	$31,500	$32,000	$33,500
4	$29,000	$29,500	$30,000	$30,500	$32,000	$32,500	$34,000
5	$29,500	$30,000	$30,500	$31,000	$32,500	$33,000	$34,500
6	$30,250	$30,750	$31,250	$31,750	$33,250	$33,750	$35,250
7	$31,000	$31,500	$32,000	$32,500	$34,000	$34,500	$36,000
8		$32,250	$32,750	$33,250	$34,750	$35,250	$36,750
9		$33,000	$33,500	$34,000	$35,500	$36,000	$37,500
10		$33,750	$34,250	$34,750	$36,250	$36,750	$38,250
11			$35,250	$35,750	$37,250	$37,750	$39,250
12			$36,250	$36,750	$38,250	$38,750	$40,250
13			$37,250	$37,750	$39,250	$39,750	$41,250
14				$38,750	$40,250	$40,750	$42,250
15				$39,750	$41,250	$41,750	$43,250
16				$41,000	$42,500	$43,000	$44,500
17					$43,750	$44,250	$45,750
18					$45,000	$45,500	$47,000

NOTES
1. There is a step increase for each year of experience.
2. There are step increases as the teacher acquires additional levels of education.
3. There are greater step levels upon achieving a master's degree and a doctoral degree.
4. Step level increases are greater after each five-year anniversary.
5. Step level increases, except for minor amounts, end at a certain anniversary if the teacher has not continued to acquire additional levels of education.
6. This is intended as a sample. You may adjust the chart according to your situation, but I would argue that the idea of building step increases of some kind for both experience and education—as well as the idea of a salary chart itself—is essential.
7. What this chart does not include but should be considered would be step increases for quality of performance. You could make each level a range of base salaries; for

example, at year five with an MA your band could be $32,500–$34,00, and award somewhere on that band according to some kind of performance matrix.

8. Remember hat these numbers are not intended as recommendations. Indeed, it should be your goal to increase these numbers as much as possible.

Now add to that salary a minimum of 50 percent for additional responsibility, an addition that would now mean a salary of $61,925. Now add compensation for an additional two months, a factor of 16.6 percent. Thus your head of school should earn a minimum salary of $72,205.

Let me add, and emphasize, one final thought on head of school compensation. A school could, and many times should, increase the 50-percent figure to 60 or even 70 percent, depending on several factors: the quality of the individual, the unique gifts he or she brings to the task, the size and complexity of the school, a history of prior success in leadership roles, and (to a certain extent) market realities. When engaged in a search process or thinking about ensuring a long-term commitment from a current head of school, a board must consider those facts. Great leaders are hard to find; that is why nearly everyone is looking. And schools want great leaders for a simple reason. Excellence produces excellence. Hire the best to achieve the best.

Determining fringe benefits

Although important, fringe benefits are an expensive part of any compensation package. In recent years, for example, health insurance rates have increased dramatically. You must, therefore, shop carefully for the best possible combination of coverage and cost. Sometimes you can offer your staff a variety of options that are based on coverage limits or shared costs. You should also consider providing a number of other fringe benefits to your faculty and staff: group life insurance, sick leave, retirement, continuing education, long-term disability, and (for twelve-month employees) vacation. I encourage schools to provide fringe benefits as generously as possible.

I would like to offer a final thought on the compensation portion of your budget. I always suggest when possible to consider outsourcing. Remember that your primary mission focuses on educational activities, not accounting or facility-maintenance activities. It makes sense, therefore, to consider outsourcing tasks such as tuition collection, payroll, cleaning, and building maintenance. Contact other area schools and businesses to see how they handle those tasks. Then contact potential contractors and compare the cost of outsourcing with the cost of providing those services in-house.

Facilities Expenses

Although compensation by far makes up the largest percentage of your budget, you still have other large monthly expenditures, and you probably see the largest expenditures going toward your facilities. In my proposed budget structure, I place those costs in the category of plant operations.

Schools face some fixed facilities expenses such as rent, lease payments, or a monthly mortgage. Some expenses—such as utility costs, building maintenance, and landscaping—vary from month to month. Every school needs to schedule some costs into its budget to fund regular preventive maintenance and depreciation replacement. These costs, for example, would go toward painting, facility upkeep and repair, and equipment repair and replacement.

Schools that do not develop a long-term facility-maintenance schedule will inevitably find themselves facing major or minor repair or replacement costs for which they have not prepared. At this point those schools must take one of three actions, all of which result in negative consequences.

School leaders might decide to delay the necessary repair or replacement. That decision brings to mind again the saying from an old commercial for Fram oil filters: "Pay me now, or pay me later." And the pay-me-later cost is always much, much higher. Delay repairing the roof on your gym and you may end up replacing the floor as well.

When delay doesn't make sense, and it seldom does, school leaders might seek to find the money without using normal budget channels—by either going to a donor or seeking a loan at a local bank. Neither is typically a good idea.

When you approach donors for help with unanticipated problems, you do two things. First, if they are willing to give you the money, you are using their gift in a reactive way. Doing so keeps many schools from ever moving ahead on strategic initiatives. Second, you are sending a negative message to your donor or donors. You are telling them that you don't know how to plan well. Borrowing, even if you can get approval for a loan, is even more problematic because, as I've already noted, it is always unwise to burden your operational budget with capital debt.

To avoid these problems, consider three things. First, conduct regular building audits. Buildings age. They take a beating. They need care. Contract with a reputable builder to come in annually and examine your buildings so that you can better predict what projects you will need to tackle in the coming year or two. You will reduce surprises dramatically. Second, always account for depreciation, which all accounting rules require anyway. Finally, establish a contingency fund. Every board should require such a fund. The percentage may vary, but you should set aside a minimum of 5 percent of your annual budget for unexpected contingencies.

For those of you who will argue, "We just can't afford to do something like that," remember my Fram oil filter illustration. You will pay. The only question is, How much more will you pay because you had to borrow the money from the bank rather than from yourself through a contingency fund?

Rent, lease, or purchase—which is the best option? Sooner or later every school will need to answer this question. Frankly I don't think we can declare a single correct answer. If, for example, your school is currently sponsored by a church that continues to strongly support Christian schooling and that will provide adequate facilities for your program, then it would make little sense to seek another option.

However, if you are on your own, you might want to consider other options. If you lead a new school, you will almost certainly be taking the best approach by finding a facility that you can rent or lease. You may face some challenges since few buildings are constructed with a school in mind. But given the current financial situation, you could probably find a church or a commercial property that would make sense for the short term.

If you do rent or lease a property, hire an attorney to draw up the contract. You must establish absolute clarity regarding who bears responsibility for what regarding utilities, repairs, access, liability, and limitations on use of the building. Don't rely on a handshake. I love the old proverb that a ragged pen is better than a good memory.

Once you have secured a location, you have time to develop a plan. Remember, neither wishing nor hoping creates the basis for a sound strategy for building toward a strong future. Wise action results from sound planning by thoughtful people fully committed to excellence. You need faith, but if you have faith divorced from wisdom, you have just more of that wishing and hoping that tends to lead to bad decisions—decisions that can saddle schools with a debt load that becomes a crushing burden. I've seen that scenario up close too many times.

Other Expenses

Most of your remaining expenses will support your instructional mission. Make choices that fit your mission. Negotiate hard for the best possible price on anything you purchase. Don't ever accept the first bid. Be reasonable, but always push a little. Remember, you can sometimes find a far better deal by buying used rather than new—not always, especially concerning technology, but probably when buying furniture.

Before you make any purchase decision, educate yourself as fully as you can. Set the goal of finding the best product at the best price. Research is better than regret any day. Talk to trusted friends and use the search engine on your computer. Dig deep. If you are an educated consumer, you will save a lot of money and reduce your frustration to a minimum.

It also makes sense to build relationships with companies that provide both services and goods. If you find the lowest price, you may not have found the best price because you will find that good relationships can be priceless. And consider that good service requires quality people. Sometimes a company charges more because that company has the best people. And it has the best people for two reasons: the company is a good place to work, and the company treats its employees well and compensates them well. Think about it. That is exactly how I've been encouraging you to think about your faculty and staff. Makes sense, doesn't it?

A Final Thought

You will not always find the solution by spending more money. If you want the school you lead to become and remain remarkable, you make the choice to hire the best staff, and you make the choice to commit, along with your staff, to do remarkable things at less cost.

Better for less is the idea behind a concept called value innovation. Let me recommend a wonderful book titled *Blue Ocean Strategy* (Kim and Mauborgne 2005). I think it will open your eyes to a different way of thinking about how to elevate your performance as a school without breaking the bank or raising your tuition to unhealthy levels.

I probably could have included a number of other topics in this chapter, but I think you have enough ideas to trigger your creative juices. Now we need to move on to the next part of the budgeting process. How do we pay for all we believe we need to do to deliver our mission with excellence?

Chapter Ten
Somebody's Got to Pay

A ll Christian school leaders in the United States and around the world face the same challenge: they are all passionately pursuing a vision that shapes nearly every aspect of their lives. It is a powerful, compelling, worthwhile vision. However, it is a vision that requires significant personal sacrifice, bundles of creative energy, and enormous financial resources.

None of those requirements is easy. We do, however, have open access to a fairly unlimited amount of personal sacrifice and creative energy if we choose to make that investment. The enormous financial-resources piece—now that problem is a bit more daunting. We must, however, eventually solve it. If not, quite frankly I think our ability to provide quality Christian schooling is at tremendous risk. As we begin to puzzle over how best to solve this funding problem, I want you to keep in mind this thought: *somebody's got to pay*. What we want and need to do comes with a cost—a rather large cost—and somebody's got to pay.

Affordable or Accessible?

In chapter 9 we looked in some detail at the first step in the budgeting process: developing expense assumptions. You face a bit of a test when developing them. But developing them is considerably easier than trying to figure out how to pay for what you want to buy, a challenge somewhat like the one we face every Christmas.

It also reminds me of one of my favorite cartoons, which features a man sitting at his desk with a deer-caught-in-the-headlights look on his face.

He punches the button on his intercom and asks his secretary, "Mrs. Jones, would you bring me a simple, obvious problem to solve?" I guarantee you that he does not have in mind funding a Christian school.

I would like you to ponder this number for a moment: $350,000. Any guesses about what that number represents? I consider $350,000 a fairly good estimate for the cost of educating a child who enters a Christian school in kindergarten and stays in a private Christian school through graduation from college. Do I have your attention?

That is a pretty big number, but I based it on some fairly sound figures. At present an ACSI member school charges on average a bit less than $5,000 a year (Smitherman n.d.). I searched the websites of several Christian colleges and found that the total charges for tuition and room and board averaged around $35,000 per year. Factor in probable tuition increases over the next fifteen years and you will arrive at around $350,000. That is a huge investment for any family. And remember, we are talking about one child.

Here is my point. Education by its very nature is simply not affordable, and the problem is going to worsen unless something truly unexpected takes place. The cost of education continues to increase at astounding rates. Even in the midst of one of the worst economic downturns in the past fifty years, tuition at U.S. public colleges increased by an average of 7.9 percent and private colleges by 4.5 percent in 2009/2010 (Gordon 2010).

But why can't we just hold the line on tuition? Why don't we just freeze the price? Simple answer: you can't. Costs never just stand still. Some of you may be old enough to remember the disastrous wage-and-price freeze during the Nixon administration. It didn't work for the federal government, and it won't work for a school. There are simply too many forces beyond anyone's control that prevent it from working.

Rather than trying to keep prices "affordable," I would argue that we need to find ways to keep Christian schooling accessible. Now I don't mean that we should simply ignore the cost problem. On the contrary, I think we should do all we can do to keep costs as low as possible.

I don't think, however, that we ought to ignore our fundamental obligation to compensate our faculty and staff in an appropriate manner. Nor should we fail to invest adequately in the infrastructure necessary to deliver our mission in a quality way. If we fail at either, we will eventually put the entire enterprise of Christian schooling at risk.

So let's set about developing our income assumptions and then directing those income assumptions toward the appropriate expenses. As we begin, I'd ask you to remember a key premise of this book: everything is connected. Thus my goal is to help you develop a comprehensive, integrated approach to funding your school. In this chapter that premise grows increasingly important.

Income Categories

Christian schools typically generate income from the following categories:
- Net tuition revenue
- Revenue from fees
  - Book
  - Activity
  - Enrollment/reenrollment
  - Facility
  - Athletic
  - Technology
  - Other
- Auxiliary-program revenue
  - Summer school
  - Summer camp and other enrichment programs
  - Food service
  - Before- and after-school care
  - Other
- Resource-development revenue
  - Fund-raising activities
    ○ Product sales
    ○ Events
  - Annual fund
  - Capital campaign

I suspect that most of those categories are fairly self-explanatory, but I'll provide just a bit of clarification.

By net tuition revenue I mean the income you receive after you have subtracted all nonfunded tuition discounts. By revenue from fees I mean all the income you produce from charging parents for any number of activities you seek to fund outside of tuition revenue. By auxiliary revenue I mean the revenue generated through all the activities and programs your school sponsors but that do not directly relate to your educational mission.

For the most part I am not a fan of charging fees in addition to tuition. Parents don't like them for the same reason that people don't like airline baggage fees. Fees just don't seem fair. Besides, parents don't like the feeling of being nickeled-and-dimed to death.

I do believe that charging fees makes sense in two situations. First, I think schools act wisely when they charge fees for enrollment and reenrollment because those fees force parents to think seriously about the commitment they have made to the school. Second, I think it is acceptable to charge fees for activities that benefit only specific students involved in specific activities. To charge a fee for something that benefits all students doesn't, however, make sense. Tuition should cover costs for those activities or materials.

For the present I'll make just two simple comments about resource development. First, Christian school leaders in general don't understand resource development nearly as well as they should and must. Second, if those leaders don't further develop their understanding, Christian schools will increasingly be at risk. This is a do-or-die issue.

Some Key Definitions

Operational costs result from all the things you must do in order to operate your school daily. They include compensation costs, facilities costs, insurance costs, instructional costs, cocurricular costs, office supply costs, basic resource-development costs, and costs associated with marketing, student recruitment, and student retention.

Program-enhancement or program-development costs include any significant expenditure designated to specifically improve the quality of a particular program at your school. Those expenses include major equipment and technology purchases, vehicle purchases, classroom improvements, and improvements to playgrounds or athletic fields.

Capital-project costs and some large program-enhancement costs fall under the category of capital costs. The difference between them is essentially one of size and scope. Equipping a biology lab falls under the classification of a program-enhancement project. If you undergo construction of a building in which to house that lab, you are engaging in a capital project, which a school should typically fund through a capital campaign.

You may be asking yourself, "Why are these definitions—or perhaps a better word would be *distinctions*—important?" If so, you are asking a good question that I'll now try to answer.

Key Revenue Streams

Let me begin with an illustration. Had you visited my grandfather's ranch in Texas with me when I was a child, you would have discovered that water was a valuable commodity, one never taken for granted. Water didn't just magically appear by turning the tap.

All the water on the ranch came from wells scattered about the property, each one serving a specific purpose. The house obviously needed a well. An old-fashioned windmill pumped the water from that well, and a water tank stored the water for those days when the wind didn't blow hard enough to turn the blades on that windmill.

But you could find those other wells at strategic locations around the property. One well, for instance, provided water near the pens where my grandfather would take his livestock at certain times of the year. Another well out in the back part of his pasture provided water for his livestock in those times when the creek was running low. Each of those three wells met a different need.

Those three wells represent how I want you to think of your budget. I want to encourage you to create three budgets. First, create an operational budget. It will cover all the costs I have previously associated with operations. You will spend the largest percentage of your revenue in this budget, for which you will use the full budget structure from chapter 9.

Second, create a program-enhancement, or program-development, budget. A totally separate source of revenue—a second well, so to speak—will fund this budget. You will use money from this source to fund expenses identified with program enhancement and development.

Your third budget will cover any capital-project expenses; as with the other two budgets, a totally separate source will fund it. Three budgets, three separate sources, and don't mix the sources. Each budget should stand alone on its ability to draw necessary resources from its designated source.

You are probably tempted to ask this question: "Can you never use water from one well to cover the need elsewhere?" The answer is that of course you can, but only as long as you don't make a habit of doing so.

One summer on my grandfather's ranch, the well outside my great-aunts' kitchen collapsed, so we had to take many long trips in the hot sun to and from a spring down on the creek several hundred yards from the house. Carrying bottles of water by hand worked, but my great-aunts saw it as a strictly short-term solution. The long-term solution required repair work on the collapsed well.

"OK, Dr. Pue. Interesting scenario. But here's my question: Which well serves which budget?" You've asked the right question. In one sense all the water from each well comes from the same source, the underground water table. (We'll touch on that metaphor a bit later.) In another sense each well, as an independent source of water, serves its own purpose. So let's address each of our wells that way; let's connect each source to its specific purpose.

Well 1

You have probably read and heard much about cost-based tuition. The conversation has been essential. In short, cost-based tuition is based on the premise that a school should set tuition rates in such a way that they generate sufficient revenue to cover the total cost of operating the school. This argument is sound. A school is acting unwisely when it purposely builds a deficit into its operational budget. Note here that I speak of a school's operational budget.

Few schools actually fund all their expenses through revenue generated solely from tuition and fees. Harvard doesn't. Your local state university doesn't. Nor does the local prep school down the street, the one that charges $16,000 per year, which, by the way, is the national average for K–12 private schools in the United States (Council for American Private Education). None of them do. Nor should you. Why not? Because you have expenses that fall outside the category of operational expenses. As we have noted, you have program-enhancement expenses and capital-project expenses. Separate wells should fund those expenses.

Schools generate the resources that come out of Well 1 in the following ways: net tuition revenue, fees, auxiliary revenue, and a designated percentage of revenue produced from investments or endowments. I would argue that schools should use this last source of revenue for specific purposes such as providing scholarships or funding operational costs associated with specifically designated programs.

That approach should help facilitate an understanding of the term *cost-based tuition*. The important thing to understand is this: schools should not use resources generated through fund-raising activities to cover operational costs, and the reason is simple. Donors quickly grow weary of requests to pour money into the black hole of any organization's operational budget. Donors will first grow weary, then they will grow distant, and then—poof—they will disappear.

Raising money to fund operational expenses is a grueling activity doomed to create only increasing frustration and an ever-expanding list of former donors. You can compare that funding strategy to pouring water into a bucket whose bottom is full of holes.

In practical terms, raising money for operational expenses also makes it difficult, perhaps impossible, to ever build a strong, sustainable, and expanding support team. You end up spending nearly all your efforts finding new supporters to replace old supporters, and you typically gain a net zero. You will normally face some replacement, but you shouldn't be spending a majority of your time seeking new supporters; you would be spending your effort more wisely by deepening current relationships and building additional ones.

Well 2

The efforts of your resource-development department should generate the resources from Well 2, and those resources should fund all those crucial program-enhancement and program-development projects that often remain nothing more than unrealized visions.

Projects of this kind typically suffer one of two fates. First, they may suffer from the "let's talk about how important this is and then mourn the financial realities that will keep us from doing what we all know we need to do" fate. Second, these projects may suffer from the "we are going to ram this thing through no matter what even if it means we have to borrow the money and burden the operational budget with capital debt" fate. This fiscally irresponsible approach will make school leadership more reluctant to pursue future projects. And often after a school spends the money, the school cannot sustain the program because the school used unrealistically low cost projections to build support in budget discussions. This is the worst possible scenario.

Give someone the choice between turning on the lights and transforming your science program, and guess which one will probably receive the strongest support. It isn't that your donors don't understand the importance of turning on the lights. They do. They just believe you address your utility bill best through tuition. If you begin to focus your thinking and energy toward funding your daily costs through tuition while funding your vision through some form of giving strategy, you will see more of your dreams come to life while building an ever-stronger donor base.

Well 3

Most schools will eventually need to engage in a major capital project, often to fund the expansion or renovation of facilities—the kind of project that usually comes with a cost in the seven- or even eight-figure range. When someone presents a proposal of this kind, people will respond in fairly predictable ways.

The visionary, typically the head of school or the chair of the board, will argue passionately that the cause of Christ is at stake if the school doesn't do something. The resident skeptic will contend with equal passion, "We've done a great job with our current resources and can continue to do so far into the future, a future that will be at risk if we try to bite off a project of this size."

Then the person of faith will say something such as, "If this is the plan that God has for the school, we need to move ahead because He will supply the necessary resources." Next will come the clear-eyed pragmatist, who will argue for a thorough feasibility study. Most will agree that some kind of study would make sense until they discover what a quality study will cost. Then those present will go off on another line of argument about the value of feasibility studies, and at least one person will ask, "Can't we just do it ourselves?" I may be exaggerating a bit, but just a bit.

Here is the reality, however. Sooner or later most schools will experience the need to find additional space, build additional space, or renovate current space, and space always comes at a price—a price somebody's got to pay.

Unfortunately, schools will often take a portion of the money necessary to fund a project from several wells at the same time. Those schools will first try to raise the money. They should try doing exactly that. But if they haven't done enough work in digging the well deep enough, they will drain all the water and discover they still do not have enough. Then they'll look for another well. Their search will probably succeed, but the well they find will be on another person's property. This person, let's call her the banker, will be happy to provide them with the water they need—at a price. So where does that leave the school? I hope you are beginning to get the picture.

Remember that one of our first principles of finance is this: never burden the operational budget with capital debt. Unfortunately, schools often do this when they decide to undertake capital building projects. When a school chooses that approach it must draw water from Well 1. Often, however, in doing so, the school pushes the capacity of Well 1 beyond its limits. To cover what can be a significant level of monthly expense, a school must then raise tuition—not to cover operational costs but to cover capital costs.

Finding capital resources is a huge topic, beyond the scope of this chapter. I have included several books on this important subject in appendix B at the end of this book. Here let me reiterate the key point I want to make. You need to draw from separate resources to fund the three separate budgets.

The Underground Reservoir

When you dig a well, you are searching for some kind of underground source of water. Even if you find a pocket of water, it will sooner or later run dry unless an even larger body of underground water is feeding it. The same applies as you seek to develop sustainable sources of funding.

Regarding Well 1, parents will be the primary funding source. These will be parents who believe your school provides the absolutely best answer for the ongoing education of their children. To ensure that continuing source of parents, you must deliver a remarkable education that actually does provide the best answer for a growing number of families.

You also need to develop a sound strategy for telling the story of this remarkable education to an ever-widening audience of people who will hopefully find your story compelling. It is through a compelling marketing strategy (another huge topic) that schools are best able to tell their story. As with budgeting and finance practices, however, school leaders are seldom adequately equipped to lead marketing efforts. Two things are thus necessary. First, school leaders would benefit from learning more about marketing. Second, it is important to identify and recruit someone to help develop, implement, and oversee effective marketing strategies at your school.

You cannot view quality marketing (or quality resource development) as an optional task. Quality marketing is essential to a healthy future for your school. Nor can you nibble away at it. Your school must market itself with both skill and excellence. Poor marketing is like a poor diet. The latter is better than starvation, but sooner or later it will make you sick. If you want to keep Well 1 from running dry, your school must have a compelling story well told.

Well 1 will over time help feed both Well 2 and Well 3, but only if you keep developing relationships with those parents who have made the choice to place their children in your school. Relationship building shouldn't end when a child graduates from your school. For sure the relationship may not be as intense for a time, but you should work hard at staying in contact with parents and students.

Most Christian schools would today be far more financially healthy if they had undertaken one relatively simple task: maintaining strong relationships with their graduates and the families of their graduates. But obviously if students upon graduation take with them only a diploma and not some wonderful memories as well, their school may find it difficult to maintain any kind of meaningful relationship.

Is the Price Right?

As important as it is to build strong resource-development programs, one reality still confronts you every time you set out to build your budget. Tuition generates nearly all your yearly income. Indeed, according to research conducted by the Association of Christian Schools International, tuition accounts for 85 percent of all income generated in the average member school (Smitherman n.d.).

Given that percentage, doesn't it make sense to ensure that you base your decision making about tuition on something more substantial than deciding how much to increase tuition above last year's rate? I think so, and because I do, I'll invest some time here discussing the importance of pricing your school right. When you price your school by setting the tuition rate for a given year, in essence you are telling people, "This tuition rate represents what it costs us to provide your children a truly exceptional education."

Let's begin by examining some realities. As I noted earlier, few costs have risen faster over the last twenty years than the cost of education. Those increased costs create such a challenge for so many families not only because those costs have risen dramatically but also because those costs have risen faster than income. Simply put, families must invest a higher percentage of household income to keep their children in your school than was necessary twenty years ago.

And not only have costs risen, but so has the debt of the average American (Money-Zine.com 2006–2011). In a sense we have somewhat of a perfect storm at work. Prices are rising rapidly, as is household debt. Income, however, has risen more modestly, as has the willingness of people to make the sacrifice necessary to keep their children in a Christian school. Sometimes, however, even the willingness to sacrifice isn't enough.

All that I've said, however, doesn't change a basic reality you cannot ignore. Education is expensive, and somebody's got to pay. The money necessary to fund that quality education you want to deliver must come from one source or another, and, like it or not, most schools still rely on tuition as their primary source of revenue.

So, I think it wise to spend some time considering this issue. In doing that, I will probably challenge some cherished assumptions and some long-held practices. You might be tempted to push my arguments aside. Please resist the impulse to do so. Agree or not, a good argument may help in working through this important topic.

Some Typical Arguments

We must primarily focus on the price point

Have you ever heard anyone say the following? "If we are not careful, we'll price ourselves out of the marketplace." I'll bet you have. You may even have said something similar yourself. And the statement has an element of truth.

You must remember, however, that Americans tend to invest their money according to what they value. So although you can't charge just any price, you must also realize that more than just price influences the decision to purchase nearly anything. Besides, people who buy on price alone will always be on the lookout for a better deal. They will never be loyal to you.

You should be able to sell your school on the basis of its reputation, programs, and core values, not on the basis of price alone. In fact, in the absence of any other information, most people assume that the more they pay for something, the better it is. So in the minds of people, low price equals low quality. You act unwisely when you feed that perception.

We must constantly scan our primary competition

In reality, your primary competition is the local public school down the street or the local charter school that sells itself as the stealth Christian school or the family who decides to homeschool. What do all those options have in common? You got it—they are free. If you are trying to compete on the basis of price, how do you compete with what is free? You can't.

So if you can't compete on the basis of price, on what basis must you compete? Here we are back again to a discussion of the power of your purpose, the quality of your program, and the unmistakable impact you make in the lives of children. If you have a compelling purpose and an exceptional program that prepares kids to successfully take on the world intellectually, spiritually, and professionally, you will always be able to compete even against something that is absolutely free.

We must remain affordable

You may believe that you must remain affordable, but, as I've tried to argue, education by its very nature is not affordable. Add personnel costs to facilities costs to program costs to capital costs and you come up with a very large number. Certainly you should make every effort to keep your costs as reasonable as possible. In trying to do so, you are simply practicing wise stewardship. Accessibility, however, is, in my opinion, a better goal than affordability.

When I was a head of school, we had a very simple policy. Anyone who truly desired a genuine Christian education and who qualified academically could attend Pike Creek Christian School irrespective of the student's financial situation. Now, we never gave away education for no charge; everyone had to pay something. But we also never turned a student away simply because the family did not possess the means to pay the tuition. Because of that policy, our school developed a scholarship program. Note I said scholarship program, not discount program.

Let me ask one additional question. At what price do you think most parents in your community would consider you affordable? Research conducted on behalf of ACSI asked that exact question. Here is the answer that emerged. Parents who would consider a Christian school option for their children but who had chosen the local public school instead said they might be tempted to make the Christian choice for $2,000 per year (Herbert Research 2005). How long could you keep your doors open if you charged $2,000 per year? Not long, I suspect—not unless you have developed that underground stream of revenue we just discussed. People really don't understand what it costs to educate their children. Thus it becomes one of your jobs to educate parents about the real costs of providing a quality education.

If we keep tuition low, people will be more likely to give gifts to the school

One of the greatest misconceptions in the Christian school world is that people will be more likely to give gifts to a school if it keeps tuition low. Most of your parents have a service-provider relationship with you; you provide the service, and they pay for the service. Not all your families have that perspective, but the overwhelming majority do.

Remember, at whatever level you set your tuition, you are sending this message: "This is what it costs to educate your child." So when you come back later and ask parents to help bridge the gap, they will probably not respond even if they can. Yes, some will; most, however, won't. When you talk about the gap, they may hear you, they may even believe you, but they just won't have enough motivation to give.

I am sure that some of you disagree with me on this point. You would like to tell me about all the money your school raises every year to fund the gap, about the generosity of your families and of your school's key friends in responding to a real need. I know that people give to help schools in such situations. But I know something else. You cannot sustain that method of funding, and it isn't the right solution to developing a strong, sustainable financial foundation for your school. Sooner or later those who are giving to your school will experience donor fatigue. When you continually appeal to donors on the basis of emotion or financial crisis, you will simply wear them out. They will do what you do. And be honest; don't you get weary of hearing the same appeals from the same ministries over and over again? Sooner or later, the appeals become nothing more than background noise.

Our past tuition levels have been on target

It is probably not the case that your tuition levels have been on target in the past. Few Christian schools have historically priced themselves appropriately. Think about it this way. How do those in leadership at Toyota set the price for their vehicles? Do they build the vehicle and then ask, What will people pay for this vehicle? Of course not. They will, of course, do market research to determine price points for different markets. They know, for example, that young people fresh out of college have a different price point than do people who are experiencing their peak earning years. So the decision makers for Toyota ensure that vehicles designated for each of those market segments are coming off the Toyota assembly lines.

For the fresh-out-of-college buyer, they'll build a Corolla. For the peak-earning-years buyer, they'll build a Camry or even their luxury brand, a Lexus. Here is the key, however. They won't build either a Corolla or a Camry and sell it for less than it costs them to build it. If they used that pricing strategy, they would soon go out of business.

In one sense many Christian schools use exactly that sure-to-fail pricing strategy as their approach. They don't do the research necessary to discover what the marketplace really wants. Rather, they assume they know on the basis of nothing more than poorly tracked anecdotal evidence. They then set a price on the basis of what they think the market will bear, but they are again armed with nothing more than anecdotal evidence. The price they set is far less than it actually costs them to deliver their service, and then are amazed that they struggle financially.

To further make my point, imagine with me for a second that you have just bought a new Camry. After driving it for a few months, you receive a letter from those in leadership at Toyota. In that letter they share with you that they are struggling a bit financially because for the last year they have been selling their cars for less than it costs to build, market, sell, and distribute them. So here is their request: Would you send in a gift to help make up that difference?

Now imagine your response to that letter. How likely is it that you would sit down and write a check? Not very, I suspect. But, you might argue, buying a car is different from paying for an education. Well, of course it is different. But many of your parents see the dynamics as much more similar than you probably want to admit. Remember, most parents view you as a service provider. They will pay the amount you charge as long as they receive something they value in return.

Setting Tuition

If, as I have been arguing, most Christian schools don't do a very good job of setting tuition rates, then what might be a better approach? In one sense you face a simple task when you set tuition. First, determine all your operational costs and then subtract projected fee income and projected auxiliary-program income. Then take that number and divide it by your predicted enrollment number. You should set that figure as your tuition rate for the coming year.

Let's say that you have put together an operational budget of $1,100,000. Now, let's say that you project fee income at $25,000 and auxiliary-enterprise income at $75,000. Then take the total of those two numbers, $100,000, and subtract that total from your projected operational-budget total of $1,100,000. That leaves you with $1,000,000 to fund from tuition. See figure 6.

Let's assume an enrollment of 250 students. Now divide your $1,000,000 cost by your 250 students and you come up with $4,000. It really is that simple. All the various pricing and discount plans make it complex.

Figure 6: Illustration for Setting Tuition	
Projected *operational* costs	$1,100,000
Subtract	
• Projected income from fees	$25,000
• Projected net auxiliary revenue	$75,000
• Subtotal	$100,000
Net	$1,000,000
Projected enrollment	250
Proposed tuition	$4,000

Notes
1. Tuition is determined by dividing net revenue (gross revenue minus income from fees and net auxiliary revenue) by the total projected enrollment.
2. Numbers will vary widely from one school to another. This is given as an illustration of the process.

Most schools have one pricing plan for elementary school, another for middle school, and yet another for high school. Then they have automatic discounts for families who have more than one enrolled child, for local pastors, and for the school staff.

I'd like you to consider a basic principle: *Avoid all automatic discounts and all different pricing plans.* Every student who attends your school should pay the same tuition as every other student who attends your school. You should create only one exception: students who demonstrate legitimate financial need.

A scholarship program should address those legitimate needs. You should put in place a formal application process for those seeking financial aid, and that process should mirror the one that families must use to apply for college financial aid. A third party should then evaluate applications by using an objective means for determining genuine need. Colleges and universities have employed this approach for decades. Why would you do it any differently? Really, why would you?

Now come all the "buts." But it costs more to educate a high school student. But our teachers are so underpaid; they deserve a discount. But parents who have more than one enrolled child will find it difficult to make tuition payments. But if we discount tuition for pastors, they will recommend the school to members of their church.

It may indeed cost more to educate a high school student than a third grader. It also costs more to educate a college senior than a college freshman, but colleges and universities charge the same tuition rates for seniors and freshmen. Why? Because those schools believe that students who enter as freshmen will stay through their senior year and thus experience all the benefits of attending that particular school. The same applies to your students.

Yes, your teachers are underpaid. You should not, however, create an unequal pay scale to solve that problem. Consider this scenario. You have two elementary teachers who have identical academic backgrounds, identical levels of experience, and identical performance ratings. Yet one receives a compensation of $25,000 per year, and the other $35,000. So one is receiving a $10,000 after-tax bonus. What is the difference? One is a single teacher, and the other has a spouse and two children who attend your school. How is that scenario equitable?

How about those multichild discounts? Why are they a problem? First of all, the discounts assume financial need when none may exist. Not every family who has more than one child in a Christian school struggles financially. And in many cases a family who has one student will struggle more than a family who has two or more students.

Second, when you offer multichild discounts, you end up asking every family who has one enrolled child to subsidize all the families who have more than one enrolled child. In essence you are asking all the parents who do not have multiple enrolled children to make an involuntary gift. In economic terms, we call that forced redistribution of wealth. Think about that.

I would suggest a simple exercise for your leadership team. (See figure 7.) Identify your highest tuition rate. That rate is typically for a high school student from a family who has only that student in your school. Take that rate and multiply it times your total full-time enrollment. Now subtract from that figure the amount of your projected tuition revenue for the current year. I'm assuming you will be able to subtract the one number from the other because of your discounts.

Now compare the resulting number with the gap you built into your budget. I find most of the time that the difference is equal to or even greater than the gap. Are you surprised? Most people are because they have never figured the real cost of offering all their discounts. It is a real cost with real consequences for your budget. In most cases you can eliminate your gap without increasing your tuition by simply eliminating your discounts. Think about it.

Figure 7: Illustration for Cost of Tuition Discounts		
Highest tuition rate (usually a single child in high school)	$7,500	
Multiply by total enrollment	400	
Projected tuition income	$3,000,000	
Subtract your current projected tuition revenue	$2,600,000	
Total discounts	$400,000	**Projected gap?**
Notes 1. This exercise will allow you to accurately assess the cost of offering tuition discounts. 2. It is often the case that the size of the discount equals the size of the gap built into the budget that must then be covered through some form of fund-raising effort.		

From a practical point of view, you would probably be acting unwisely by just eliminating all your discounts. It would make sense, however, to begin the process by decreasing the amount of those discounts each year over about five years until you have eliminated all the discounts. You will face the greatest challenge in eliminating the discounts you offer your teachers. I still think you have to try. From a budgeting point of view, teacher discounts are an uncontrollable, a fact I noted when discussing first principles. That variable could create havoc with your budget. Make it simple. Raise salaries. Eliminate discounts.

Many leaders have not encountered this way of thinking about tuition. Others have wrestled with these issues for years. Some of you find merit in what I have had to say. Others disagree. I ask only that you thoughtfully consider the merits of my arguments. In the end the responsibility for funding your schools falls not to me but to you. My goal is to encourage you to think about some different approaches to a common challenge.

Final Thoughts on Tuition

Inclusive tuition

As I have argued, I believe that you act wisely when you set your tuition so that it covers all reasonable operational expenses. Therefore, you should avoid, when possible, all extra charges. If, however, you are intent on charging fees beyond fees for enrollment/reenrollment and activities, I would limit them to these additional fees:

- *Facility fees.* Schools that charge such fees believe that every family should pay for the maintenance and replacement of the physical plant. Schools should charge these fees per family, not per student.
- *Book fees.* If a school provides textbooks, these fees would cover all initial purchases and ongoing replacements of all textbooks.
- *Technology fees.* These fees would provide for the initial purchase, ongoing maintenance, and replacement of all student-used technology.

In all cases fees should go into a fund reserved exclusively for the purpose intended upon collection. Schools should not use those monies for other purposes, and the operational budget should not absorb those monies. It is imperative that schools provide a clear rationale for each fee and give an equally clear accounting for how they use each fee.

Prorated tuition

On occasion families cannot remain in the school for an entire year. Some schools require that families pay an entire year's tuition at the beginning of the year. Others ask for quarterly or monthly payments. In any of those cases, each school should establish and publicize a prorated schedule that is based on class days marked at significant intervals such as the end of the first week, the end of the first month, and the end of the first quarter. If a family is enrolled for any part of one of those intervals, the school should charge the family for the full interval.

Delinquent tuition policy

From the very beginning your school should establish a policy for addressing delinquent tuition accounts. Your school is not helping a family if the school allows the family to remain in the school and as a consequence the family ends the year with a $4,000 bill in delinquent tuition. In addition, bad-debt losses put a strain on your budget and discourage families who stay current with their payments.

One proven way of reducing delinquent and uncollected tuition is to out-source tuition collection. Several companies provide this service. Research the market and choose one. Outsourcing allows you to focus on your core, which is education, not accounting.

Conclusion

You begin building your budget by developing your expense assumptions. Only then do you develop your income assumptions. And it is important to remember that each budget requires a different funding source. Since your primary source of revenue is tuition, you need to have a wise strategy for setting tuition rates. Do all of that well and you will be on your way to a healthier financial future.

Chapter Eleven
On the Horns of a Dilemma?

For what would you be willing to spend $36,000 a year? Indeed, I wonder how many of the people reading this chapter could afford to spend $36,000 a year on anything. That's a lot of money. In fact, for a bit less than $2,700 a month, which translates to $32,400 a year, you could make payments on a $500,000 mortgage at a rate of 5 percent. You would be living in a pretty nice house in most parts of the country.

Or you could do what a young friend of mine was asked to do this year and pay $3,000 a month in tuition to educate his three children, two in elementary school and one in middle school, at his local Christian school. For him and his wife, that cost was the breaking point. After funding a Christian school education for many years, he just couldn't continue. Instead, he and his wife currently homeschool all three children.

They didn't want to make that choice. They loved the school their children had been attending. They would have preferred keeping them in that school, but they, like an increasing number of parents, find themselves on the horns of a dilemma. Do they keep their children in the local Christian school and face the real prospect of financial ruin, or do they place their children in the local public school and deal with significant cultural, moral, and worldview challenges?

That isn't a made-up story. It entails a real family facing genuinely tough decisions right now, as we move through the second decade of the twenty-first century. And I think the problem is going to become only worse for Christian schools unless Christian school leaders respond in a truly creative manner.

To illustrate further, I would like to share part of what I recently learned from another friend who has been approached about teaching an online course at a Christian university near where he lives. This particular university was near complete collapse when three wealthy Christian investors purchased it about ten years ago. None of those investors were educators, but they were committed to building a world-class Christian university.

Today that university enrolls nearly 40,000 students: 3,000 traditional on-campus students and 37,000 nontraditional online students. The university just hired a key person from the University of Phoenix to further develop its nontraditional programs. The Christian university has an ambitious enrollment goal of 100,000 students. Only time will tell whether it will achieve this lofty objective, but it is certainly well on its way.

Now, how do these two stories connect? Give me a few paragraphs, and I think I can make the connection. Twenty years ago I doubt anyone could have imagined the possibility that any school other than a major state university could enroll anywhere near 100,000 students. That lack of vision was due in part to the real problem of space. Where would you put 100,000 students?

The model developed by John Sperling, coupled with remarkable developments in technology, enabled the University of Phoenix to solve those logistical problems (University of Phoenix). If you have any doubts, consider these staggering numbers. The University of Phoenix currently enrolls more than 400,000 students and generates over $4 billion in revenue a year (Berry 2011). No one else comes even close, at least not yet. The University of Phoenix proved the model could change. Others have followed suit.

Now the University of Colorado isn't going away, nor will Ohio State University or the University of Southern California—or Harvard and the rest of the Ivies. But, as I have observed repeatedly, the world is changing, not gradually but in quantum leaps. Those who fail to respond wisely will probably find themselves facing expulsion from the marketplace. Does that possible reality strike close to home?

Here is the connection. Christian schools, like the one you lead, are caught up in the same currents that are driving schools of all levels everywhere across the country. School leaders must rethink every component of their schools, from the instructional strategies they use all the way to how they fund their schools.

As I argued in the previous chapter, schooling by its very nature is an expensive endeavor, one that grows more costly by the year. Adding to the upward pressure on tuition, Christian school boards are increasingly committed to hiring quality faculty and staff and then compensating them in an appropriate manner.

I enthusiastically applaud those efforts. At the same time I understand not only the financial impact of those kinds of commitments but also the financial impact of the decisions to improve facilities and to keep pace with rapidly evolving technology. All those necessary improvements, however, require a lot of capital. So back to my mantra: *somebody's got to pay*. If the only answer to that question is the parents, I think more and more schools will find themselves at risk.

As strongly committed as I am to the right pricing strategy, I am equally committed to reality. And reality tells me that the number of Christian parents who can afford a $36,000 yearly tuition bill is probably pretty small. If we do nothing, I fear we will see an acceleration of withdrawals. More and more families will find another alternative, be it homeschooling or attending a charter school or even attending a virtual school. It is time to act and to act decisively.

Addressing the 85/15 Reality

Research by ACSI tells us that the average ACSI school generates 85 percent of its income through tuition and fees. All other sources of revenue produce the other 15 percent of the school's income (Smitherman n.d.). But I believe that continuing the 85/15 reality will increasingly put schools at risk. Schools must find ways to generate a larger percentage of their income from nontuition sources. It is almost a certainty that tuition will always provide the greatest percentage of a school's income. But I also believe that schools that build strong, sustainable nontuition sources of revenue in addition to using a sound pricing strategy are the schools most likely to thrive in the coming decades.

Some of you may be thinking that I argued for cost-based tuition in chapter 10 and that now I seem to be backing away from that concept. But please note that I did not argue for cost-based tuition. I proposed that revenue from three sources—tuition, fees, and auxiliary programs—should cover operational costs. I then suggested a simple approach to setting tuition.

If the number you produce by that formula is higher than you are willing to ask of your parents, you have three possible courses of action:

- You can reduce your projected expenses. You may indeed find costs you can eliminate without degrading your program's quality. But you must not blind yourself to reality in the name of keeping tuition low. Denial is a poor strategy for building a strong financial future.
- Ask yourself, Can we increase the amount of revenue we are currently generating through auxiliary programs?
- Ask yourself, How can we benefit from investment revenue generated through an endowment?

Many Christian school leaders are belatedly coming to understand the importance of building a strong resource-development program. They realize that trying to cover a built-in gap through some kind of product sale is unwise. It is time to follow the good first step with other necessary steps. Schools must eliminate the very idea of a gap and build an operational budget that is fully funded from income generated through tuition, fees, and auxiliary revenue.

Also, it is time to use creativity for increasing income from your auxiliary programs. This endeavor will require a bit of entrepreneurial thinking. Having addressed funding for your operational budget, you must then determine to build a strong annual-giving program for the purpose of both funding all program-enhancement costs and helping fund your school's financial-aid needs. Further steps involve the longer term, and will involve capital funding activities and taking first steps toward development of an endowment at your school.

I know that you must be feeling a bit overwhelmed about now. I understand your reaction. I also understand the importance of committing to an integrated, long-term funding strategy at your school. If you are like the majority of Christian school leaders, you are at the place where more and more parents are finding themselves: on the horns of a dilemma. Thus you can work to find long-term solutions to your funding dilemma, or you can ignore reality. The choice is fully yours. My goal is to encourage you to engage in some thoughtful problem solving and to give you some ideas to shape your thinking.

Thinking and Acting like an Entrepreneur

Let me begin by listing a number of possible auxiliary programs you could provide, some of which you may already provide at your school:

- Full-time daycare
- Extended care before and after school
- Hot-lunch programs
- Summer camps: music, fine arts, technology, sports, academic development
- Music conservatory
- Tutoring
- English as a second language
- Tech classes
- International-student programs
- Rental of facilities

I suspect that you could add several items to my list after just a bit of brainstorming. The point I want to make is that there are a number of nontraditional ways to generate revenue to help fund your operational costs. I also want you to consider that your school may experience benefits beyond additional revenue when offering quality auxiliary programs.

For example, ask yourself the following questions: Why do most schools offer before- and after-school care? Don't they do so because in many families both husband and wife work outside the home? Those parents must solve the problem of what to do with their children during the hours between the end of school and the time one parent arrives home from work.

Parents can solve that problem in a number of ways. They can ask their children to head to a friend's house or to a grandparent's house or even home to an empty house. They can arrange the delivery of their children from your school to a daycare. Or they can let their children's school care for their children. Which option do you think might make the most sense to the parents who have children enrolled in your school?

An entrepreneur does at least one thing very well. He or she identifies a need and then sets out to provide a way to meet that need. Someone who discovers a real need and then develops a reasonable, beneficial way to meet it will probably experience success. That is what you did when you decided to offer an extended-care program. I believe that you could solve any number of problems fully related to your primary purpose while at the same time generating much-needed revenue.

Let me offer another couple of illustrations. The problem that plagues working parents during the school year plagues them even more during the summer. Since both parents work, who will care for their children? So why don't you provide a program of care for those kids, some of whom you currently enroll?

Undoubtedly you will need to solve logistical problems if you are going to offer a summer program. If you do it well, however, the benefits will far outweigh any challenges. First of all, you have the opportunity to make an impact on children for good. Second, you can provide quality jobs for your teachers who need to work in the summer. Third, you can further enhance your teaching resources with some of the money you generate from the summer program. Fourth, you can't buy better marketing. Run a quality summer program and you will draw the interest of parents who may not even know you exist. Parents who have their children in the local public schools probably don't go looking for a place to educate their children. They will, however, go looking for a place to provide quality care during the summer.

If public-school parents choose to enroll their children in your summer program, you now have the opportunity to win the hearts of those parents. Serve their children well through a quality program delivered by caring, capable people, and you open a door you couldn't open any other way. And think about this key point: those parents will pay you to market to them. I must confess I can't think of a legitimate reason you wouldn't want to try such a program.

Here's another idea. Why don't you start a music conservatory that provides private lessons to people in your community? I have a friend who established such a conservatory at a local church in the Atlanta area. The conservatory offered lessons after school and in the evenings. Within five years, the conservatory enrolled more than 400 students, and it had attracted some of the best teachers in the community.

The success of that conservatory was no accident, however. It required a lot of work on the part of a very capable musician who also possessed a strong dose of entrepreneurialism. It also required a church willing to take a bit of a risk. The payoff has been huge for the church, which is now attracting—through a side door—people who might never have come through the front door.

Permit one final illustration. A school I have worked with faced a challenge many schools have faced. For years they had been meeting in a church building. The church did not sponsor the school, but the church graciously provided classrooms at a reasonable price.

The school's leaders realized, however, that the school needed to develop an independent identity in order to grow. To accomplish that goal, school leaders believed they needed their own facility. So they set about looking for land. Their search for property ended unsuccessfully, and that failure prompted them to approach solving the problem in a more creative way.

They began to look at commercial properties. They found a large strip mall that included a movie theater. It was far more space than they could use, but it was in an excellent location. They negotiated a good price for the property but still faced the cost of reconfiguring the buildings. The estimated price tag for the project was simply beyond their capabilities until someone came up with a truly entrepreneurial idea.

Why not purchase the building, reconfigure and refurbish the portion needed for the school, and then rent out the rest of the facility to small businesses? They did exactly that. The rental income currently covers the debt service and in time will create a strong income flow that will help fund special projects, operational costs, or the school's scholarship fund.

I don't want to make it sound easier than it is. A project like the one I just described requires a lot of work. Mistakes will occur. But anyone who starts a business must undergo hard work and mistakes. Every decision requires care and caution. You need to do your homework and seek wise counsel. Sometimes, however, we mislabel fear and call it caution or mistake the loudest voice in the room for the wisest voice in the room. In either case we fail to act when delay is not a virtue but a vice.

To make something like this take place, however, you need to work at identifying the entrepreneur in your midst. That task is easier than you think. Just look for the person who makes magic happen and does so using few resources. Look for people who won't be stopped when they hear, "There just isn't any money for that project." Look for people who respond to a "No" by asking, "If I can find the resources, can I go ahead with my idea?" People who refuse to be thwarted simply because "there is no money" can help change your school.

But Remember, You Have to Charge What It Costs

It won't do you any good, however, to think entrepreneurially if you aren't willing to act entrepreneurially. You can't just come up with good ideas for an auxiliary program. You also need to develop the program, figure the real costs of the program, and then charge the real cost plus a bit of a profit margin. You absolutely cannot offer auxiliary programs and then end up subsidizing those programs from your tuition revenue. Unfortunately, school leaders do so more than they want to admit. Consider two illustrations.

What I discover when I am given the opportunity to look closely at a school's budget often amazes me. At one school I was comparing income from its hot-lunch program with the expense of operating that program; I concluded that the school had lost over $10,000 during the previous year. Sadly but not surprisingly, no one knew. That lack of knowledge occurred in part because of the way the school developed its budget and in part because of a lack of attention to the numbers. Both are big problems. An equally significant predicament, however, was that no one had developed a business plan for the hot-lunch program. When you don't treat each component of your budget as a cost center, a similar scenario almost always occurs.

In another school I discovered an even larger problem in a program designed to help learning-disabled students. The loss in this case had exceeded $30,000 in the previous year, and it would probably be even larger in the current year. When I suggested that the school raise the rate it was charging the families served by the program, the school leaders were very resistant. When I inquired about the resistance, the school leaders told me the learning-disability program formed a core part of the school's curriculum even though it served only a small percentage of students. The school wanted to make Christian schooling available to all students.

I applauded the school leaders' commitment but still raised the question. How can you provide a service that benefits a small number of students at a loss and then ask other families to subsidize that service? Not surprisingly the school leaders had not thought of it in that way. School leaders seldom do.

I found it very interesting that the school had chosen to limit the number of students in the program despite a huge demand for the service. In the previous year the school had received nearly 300 inquires about the program yet enrolled only a few. When I inquired about why, I received two answers. First, the school didn't want to overwhelm itself with students who had learning disabilities. Second, as a discipleship school it would enroll only students from families in which at least one parent was a professing Christian.

I pressed the school leaders on both issues, but they would not increase the price they charged for essentially an auxiliary program and would not consider any creative alternatives such as offering an after-school tutoring program. So they were left with a $30,000 hole in their budget that they were trying to cover through, you guessed it, fund-raising. It didn't work. If donors are reluctant to give to cover faculty salaries, will they give to cover losses created by a poor pricing strategy in an auxiliary program? The answer is simple. They won't.

You should run your hot-lunch program like any business, as you should any program that benefits a particular classification of students. In either case you must charge enough to cover all legitimate costs. You can do that task relatively easily when dealing with hard costs. For example, if you provide a hot-lunch program, you should not have difficulty figuring such costs as staff, food, beverages, condiments, napkins, plates, plasticwear, and cups. If you stop there, however, you have missed many significant costs. The program incurs costs related to equipment such as purchase, maintenance, and replacement. What about utilities? Do you print daily or weekly menus? Does a staff person invest time coordinating volunteers who operate the hot-lunch program? Have you built any profit margin into your costs? If not, why not?

I'm not talking about the kinds of obscene profits made in certain kinds of business ventures. But you must generate enough profit to ensure that you can continue to further develop and enhance your business. Bare-bones operations don't normally survive for long.

Let me offer a simple illustration. Let's say that your hot lunch menu on one day consists of a hot dog, chips, some kind of veggie, and a beverage. Total hard costs are $1.50. In most cases a school would then charge $1.50. If a school did, it would certainly be losing money. You simply must factor in all costs before setting a price.

Four additional realities often drive the price of a product or a service: demand, quality control, inventory control, and customer service. If the program lacks demand, the program will generate insufficient revenue. The best way to create demand is to offer a quality product at a good price while serving with excellence. Does that strategy sound familiar? It is exactly the one you use in marketing your school. And remember, perception is part of the equation, as is planning.

A winsome environment invites people to join in. Make lunch special, for example, and more students will probably become customers. Make it fun, nutritious, and customer friendly, and more moms will probably become customers. And more customers generate more revenue.

You also need to practice wise purchasing and sound inventory control because what you don't spend adds to your net revenue. It might make sense to contact a few people in the food-service industry to help you learn some useful information about inventory control. The scope of what you do may be a bit less complicated, but you will probably learn some useful tips.

By the way, you will face those same kinds of issues whatever your auxiliary program. Price is important, but it is not the only issue or even the most important one. Whether people are looking for childcare, a summer program, a hot lunch, or an education for their children, they all look for quality and for exceptional service. When they find both, they will almost always stop and consider because finding both quality and exceptional service is such a rarity.

Where Next?

We have examined how a proper pricing strategy for tuition coupled with an entrepreneurial approach to auxiliary programs can fully fund a Christian school's operational budget. Now in chapters 12 and 13 we can turn our attention to the equally crucial issue of resource development in general and planned giving specifically.

Chapter Twelve
Transforming Partnerships

Four interconnected realities form the basis of any transformational partnership:

- Unwavering trust
- Passion for a common cause
- Commitment to each other's spiritual and intellectual growth
- All combined with a large dose of laughter and fun

In this chapter I plan to build on some of those ideas to help you think through how best to foster powerful partnerships of the kind that can transform your school. Let's begin that discussion with an observation and some recommendations.

The Great Disconnect

If I could recommend only one book as a foundation for thinking about resource development, I would recommend *Revolution in Generosity* (Willmer 2008). Wes Willmer and the various contributors set out to help the readers rethink their resource development worldview. This is an important task because our culture influences us more than we think and because few of us have received quality teaching on finance or stewardship issues from a sound biblical worldview framework. I have found that cultural norms rather than the Scriptures shape the thinking of many leaders of Christian organizations regarding a number of crucial issues such as finance.

As a result I fear that unbiblical, highly pragmatic thinking is engulfing us in the matter of fund-raising. We give a high five to the Scriptures, but we don't often make the Scriptures the first stop for finding answers. When the Scriptures do make an entrance, they often serve more as a tasty appetizer than the main course. In case you doubt what I am saying, let me offer a simple test.

Choose any topic related to educational life—leadership, planning, finance, marketing, instructional strategies, curriculum design—and ask yourself this question: When confronted with such an issue, where do I turn first for answers? If forced at this moment to outline, for example, a biblical approach to money, giving, and finance, could you do it? We have a subtle but real prejudice. We revere the Scriptures, but we tend to ignore them when trying to solve the "real" issues of life.

This, then, is our challenge. We can approach the legitimate need to raise money by using strategies that reflect our cultural values more than they reflect the Scriptures—strategies that may work for a time—or we can commit ourselves to a strategy of teaching and modeling in which our goal is not fund-raising or even "friend raising" but heart transformation.

Four Foundational Principles

Many Scripture passages speak to giving. Few, however, are as extensive as Paul's instructions to the church at Corinth found in 2 Corinthians 8 and 9. I recommend that you and your leadership team study those two chapters with care because in them you will find a wealth of sound biblical insight on giving. I'd like to highlight four principles from that passage.

First of all, Paul clearly identifies one primary motive for giving: gratitude for God's gift of His Son. Paul writes, "For you know the grace of our Lord Jesus Christ, that though He was rich, yet for your sake He became poor, so that you through His poverty might become rich" (2 Corinthians 8:9, NASB). In fact, as Paul reminds us, God's gift to us is so remarkable that it is beyond description (see 9:15). When we fully understand God's gift of grace, our response to such a gift can be nothing less than generous giving.

Second, as Paul instructs, we should give to meet the genuine needs of others. The offering that Paul speaks of in this passage would be used to purchase food for the members of the church in Jerusalem and the surrounding areas. The need was real, not manufactured. As followers of Christ, we can respond legitimately to genuine need in only one way—by giving generously. When we do otherwise, we distort and demean what it means to follow Jesus Christ (see 2 Corinthians 8:13–14).

Third, we give to bring glory to God. Ponder these words for a moment: "For the ministry of this service is not only fully supplying the needs of the saints, but is also overflowing through many thanksgivings to God. Because of the proof given by this ministry, they will glorify God for your obedience to your confession of the gospel of Christ and for the liberality of your contribution to them and to all, while they also, by prayer on your behalf, yearn for you because of the surpassing grace of God in you" (2 Corinthians 9:12–14, NASB).

We give no clearer evidence that we are the children of God than our love for one another, and nothing evidences love more than generous giving to meet the legitimate needs of others (see 1 John 3:16–18). If we are going to convince a skeptical world that our message of faith is real, we must do more than proclaim truth; we must also live truth (see James 2:14–17). We must, as Jesus instructs us, let our lights so shine before other people that they see our good works and as a result see the true nature of God (see Matthew 5:14–16).

Fourth, giving signals an understanding of biblical partnership, a principle we can clearly see in this passage. In fact, I don't think anyone who truly understands the Body of Christ as presented in the New Testament can ignore this concept of partnership.

Ponder for a moment the potential impact on the cause of Christ in the world if more people who claim to be His followers would reflect the heart and attitude of those in the Macedonian church. Of them Paul writes, "For I testify that according to their ability, and beyond their ability, they gave of their own accord, begging us with much urging for the favor of participation in the support of the saints" (2 Corinthians 8:3–4, NASB). Paul gives not a single hint of giving to get, of sowing seed in hope of some reward. No, these people gave simply because they could do nothing else in the face of such great need and still claim to be the transformed followers of Jesus of Nazareth.

In my experience people give for one of three primary reasons. They give because they believe they can receive something in return (a tax deduction or some other benefit). They give because they are committed to the organization—that is, they believe in the organization's purpose and potential impact. Or they give because they understand their obligation as children of God and as stewards of the resources He has entrusted to them. In that last scenario, they will give to your school or organization because they have come to trust you and value what you are doing to advance God's purposes.

Some Thoughts on Cultivating a Culture of Generosity

Richard Towner writes, "The church should be the central place for believers to come to understand biblical stewardship in a way that transforms their hearts, conforms their lives to the image of Christ, and results in overflowing generosity" (2008, 119). I fully agree. Unfortunately, however, many church leaders seem reluctant to teach the grace of giving, and the consequences are clear. As Towner observes, "Failure to address such a major issue in people's lives may be one of the greatest acts of self-marginalization in the history of the church. It also ensures that giving to God's work in the world through the local church suffers" (120–21).

Towner asks us to consider more: "Those who succumb to the materialistic pull of the culture have little motivation and few resources to offer, and God's vision for the local church goes unfulfilled for lack of financial support. Scarcity of resources creates other negative effects within the church:
- Unhealthy competition for limited resources arises between ministries.
- Those skilled in financial matters have undue influence in church affairs.
- The budget drives ministry rather than ministry driving the budget.
- Morale of staff and congregation suffers as the pressing issue becomes how the budgetary needs can be met" (2008, 121).

Do these bulleted points sound familiar? I believe, for example, that most pastors view the local Christian school, even the one sponsored by the church they pastor, as their most serious competition for limited resources. In their minds every dollar given to a Christian school is a dollar not available to fund the ministries and programs at their churches.

Instead of addressing the root of the problem, however, pastors seem willing to live with the current reality for fear of offending one church constituency or another. But the strategy of living with the current reality is failing. As Towner notes, "We are in a battle of competing ideologies, perhaps the major spiritual battle of our day—and we are losing badly" (2008, 122). I agree, and I believe we must do something constructive in response. Here are some ideas on how to proceed.

Examine Yourself

Let's be honest. Perhaps the most difficult thing for any of us to do is to peel back all the superficial layers by which we portray ourselves and to take an honest, objective look inside our hearts. I know how hard this process can be, but you simply cannot ask others to be generous if you yourself do not live a generous life. Todd Harper states that a leader cannot take people where he or she has not been (2008, 225). His observation echoes an exhortation by the apostle Paul, who boldly challenges the church at Corinth, "Follow my example, as I follow the example of Christ" (1 Corinthians 11:1, NIV).

Although taking an objective look within is very difficult, it is absolutely essential. You cannot have mixed motives. Are you trying to cultivate a culture of generosity, or are you trying to fund a particular program? Believe me when I say that people will know the difference.

Is it wrong to seek funding for a particular program? Of course not, as long as it is a worthwhile project, one that will truly advance God's purposes in the world. It is wrong, however, to ask anyone to help fund a project in which you yourself have not invested heavily, even sacrificially.

Deepen Your Understanding

I made an assertion that many in the church have a flawed worldview about money and possessions. I know I did for many years. I viewed giving as an obligation. If I met that obligation, God would bless me. If I withheld my giving, however, I could expect my car to break down or my children to become sick. God was going to get His 10 percent one way or another.

You might be shocked that anyone could ever hold such a view of God and giving. On the other hand, you might be nodding your head as you recall similar teaching. Whatever your response, however, I hope you will agree with this statement: The only effective response to error is truth, but truth is not always obvious, and it can often be the more challenging path. Error is much easier to swallow. Not only is Satan the father of lies, but he is also a master at creating them.

Because of the seductive power of a well-crafted lie, Solomon implores, "Make your ear attentive to wisdom" (Proverbs 2:2, NASB). Paul instructs Timothy, "Be diligent to present yourself approved to God as a workman who does not need to be ashamed, accurately handling the word of truth" (2 Timothy 2:15). Paul knew that finding the truth about anything requires strenuous effort. If you want to develop a biblical approach to giving, you must make the investment. At the end of this book in appendix B, I've included a list of books you may find helpful as you research this topic and deepen your understanding.

Encourage Your Team

As your understanding of giving deepens, you will want to invite your team to join you on the journey. When you do invite them, expect a bit of resistance. Most teaching on giving in a typical church in the United States takes place as a prelude to a capital campaign or as a response to a decline in giving. People may perceive such teaching as a bit manipulative. You must challenge that perspective.

More important, make every effort to cultivate a common understanding about giving among your team members. Without that understanding, any organization faces remarkable difficulty moving forward. To cultivate understanding, I would add teaching a biblical approach to finance to your yearly staff-development curriculum.

Let me address the "I don't know if that is a good idea" objection. You may be thinking, "We are an academic institution. What time I have for professional development needs to be spent helping my teachers become better educators. The church should address giving. It doesn't fall in my realm of responsibility as a head of school."

First of all, the church doesn't teach about finance or stewardship or giving, at least not often and seldom well. And when teaching does take place, it is usually through something such as a Crown Ministries class that seldom touches more than a handful of people. Rarely does a church take a systematic approach to teaching on the topic. If you don't teach your teachers, who will?

Second, everyone on your staff must understand that resource development is a team sport. They must all participate at some level in giving and in helping build appropriate partnerships. Resource development does not belong to a handful of professionals tasked with raising money. A resource professional plays an important role in coordinating, focusing, equipping, and enabling the efforts of everyone involved with the school. No one involved with the school, however, should view that person as the one who goes out and gets the money—a perspective that is the very essence of a secular approach to modern fund-raising.

Practice Organizational Generosity

Leaders who are not generous will find it difficult and perhaps impossible to ask others to demonstrate generosity. What is true of leaders is true of organizations. If giving is not woven into the fabric of your school, how can you expect others to give in generosity to you? I'm not suggesting you be unwise about scholarships, for example. You can't just give money to anyone who asks. You can, however, develop sound scholarship guidelines and respond to genuine need.

Years ago the leadership at Pike Creek adopted a policy worded something like this: "No student who truly desires a Christian school education will be denied admission to Pike Creek Christian School because of an inability to pay." The policy came with a bit of risk that required a sound structure for evaluating whether people were seeking a genuine Christian education or just looking for an alternative to their local public school.

The policy also required us, on occasion, to give away a classroom seat that could have gone to a full-paying customer. The policy, however, made sense to us in the context of generous giving. Some families simply cannot afford the kind of tuition that schools must charge.

As you develop your scholarship guidelines, I encourage you to consider using an outside agency to evaluate scholarship applications. This outsourcing takes significant pressure off you while providing an appropriately objective framework for deciding how much scholarship money to give to a particular family. You will need to consider each case by using some kind of additional internal grid that takes into account important nonfinancial contributions a particular family or student has made to your school.

Your school should not limit generosity to giving scholarships. There are other ways you can make generosity visible to students, parents, and staff while making a genuine difference in the life of someone else. What about a partnership with World Vision? How about involvement with the Angel Tree or Operation Christmas Child programs? Why not help coordinate with area churches to raise the profile of those programs or similar programs?

To further demonstrate generosity, you can participate in local community projects. Many schools already do so. Your involvement can help overcome the unfortunate stereotype that Christian schools are insular and disconnected. Your involvement also powerfully cultivates in your students a biblical understanding of what Jesus meant when He talked about giving a cup of cold water in His name. Our students need to see a life of service and generosity as a normal, natural, foundational expression of a life of faith in Jesus.

Pursue Common Cause

Now comes the really hard part. If, as I believe, most local churches view most Christian schools as competitors, and if, as I believe, that sense of competitiveness harms the cause of Christ, then we need to challenge the status quo. It won't be easy, but it must take place, and schools will probably need to take the lead.

"But," you might ask, "in what way will pursuing common cause build a culture of generosity in our school family?" In pursuing common cause, you always invest a portion of your resources in something the other person considers important. In this case the other person would be one or more local churches.

Consider mission trips as an example. Many Christian schools sponsor mission trips. So do many churches. Can you see why some people may think the school has become a competitor? Most kids must choose between one trip and another. When the student chooses the school trip instead of the church trip, how do you think the youth leaders at the church will respond? Why not meet with area youth leaders and at least explore the possibility of working together? Meeting may be worth a try, especially given all the emphasis on unity in the New Testament.

You can also pursue common cause through teaching on stewardship. Co-sponsoring either Crown Ministry classes or workshops on estate planning can easily create win-win situations for Christian schools and local churches. Sharing costs may allow you to do something substantial.

Parachurch ministries, including Christian colleges and universities, engage in very proactive estate-planning activities. Those organizations use income from estates as a primary way to fund special projects as well as endowments. Local churches and Christian schools, however, seldom receive such gifts simply because local churches and Christian schools do little, if anything, to educate their congregations and constituents about biblical stewardship. It is time to address that failure.

So why not approach local pastors to see about the possibility of working together in common cause about biblical stewardship? Will you face a challenge working together? Absolutely. However, the potential benefits to your school and to the entire community far outweigh any costs. I recommend you contact both Crown Financial Ministries at www.crown.org and Generous Giving at www.generousgiving.org to seek help in developing a strategy for working together in common cause with local churches and with other Christian schools in your community. This discussion on working together goes beyond the matter of common cause—to financial survival.

True Partnership

I can't recall the first time I heard someone say, "It isn't about fund-raising—it is about friend raising," but I know I've heard similar sentiments dozens of times over the years. That concept forms the basis for much of the literature on resource development. The key, we are told, to successful fund-raising is friend raising, so school leaders receive the advice to go out and make friends with people who have the resources to help schools achieve their mission.

I don't necessarily disagree with that advice so much as I see the potential for misunderstanding and abuse. I have learned over the years that people of wealth tend to be a bit cautious when someone shows up at their door expressing a desire to be their next best friend.

Think about it from your own perspective. How often do you add a new best friend to your list? I suspect it is somewhere between rarely and almost never. We may add new colleagues or golfing buddies with some frequency, but close friends? I don't think so. And I suspect most people are just like you. They are not really trying to add anyone to their close-friend list. When that addition occurs, it is usually a delightful surprise because, as we all know, making close friends is not easy, and there is no simple formula. Good friends are simply hard to find, and I think we somehow diminish the meaning of the word *friend* by using it loosely in the term *friend raising*.

Here's an idea I want you to consider. I don't think our primary goal in fund-raising is to make friends with people. I certainly believe that sometimes in God's providence friendships do blossom as we seek to connect with people who can help fund the mission of Christian schooling. Rather than building friendships, I think we should direct our efforts at developing true biblical partnerships.

Think of it this way. You can have a friendship with someone without ever coming together in common cause, and you can pursue a strong partnership with someone without ever becoming that person's friend. Partnership does, however, require two essential elements: trust among the partners coupled with passion for a common purpose. Thus I would argue that you must work at developing both trust and common cause when you seek to develop biblical partnerships.

Here are two things I've learned over the years about people of wealth who are Christians. First, I've learned that they tend to understand biblical stewardship better than most people in the typical evangelical church. They understand, for example, that everything belongs to God, that in one sense private ownership of property does not exist. They also understand, however, that people have personal responsibility for how they manage the resources that God entrusts to their care.

Thus people of wealth think of their support for a particular organization as investing more than as giving. The difference is crucial because people of wealth invest God's resources in Kingdom work the same way they invest in the stock market. They want to invest where they see the possibility of the greatest return. As a result, they tend to invest in ministries that repeatedly demonstrate excellence in delivering a particular mission.

They look for ministries that make wise, strategic decisions. They look for ministries that manage their resources well and hire exceptional people. When investigating a ministry, they look for absolute integrity as well as genuine impact. In other words, they look for a well-led, professionally managed ministry that makes a difference for Christ. They are less interested in what a ministry says it is hoping to do than in what they are seeing as clear evidence that the ministry has actually achieved something remarkable.

It makes me sad to write this, but I think one of the main reasons so few people of wealth regularly and substantially support Christian schools is that they just don't believe we in Christian schooling are very good at what we do. I think they see most Christian school leaders as well-meaning but marginally competent.

When I voice this observation, I often receive negative feedback from people who are selflessly investing their lives in the cause of Christian schooling. I understand the reaction. Here, however, is the problem. When school leaders do speak of impact, they tend to focus on test scores. Academic excellence makes up part of the story that Christian schools must tell. However, there is little to set Christian schools apart from any local prep schools if Christian school leaders make academic excellence the central ingredient of their message. Christian schools must represent what Jim Collins and Jerry Porras call the genius of the And (1997).

Christian schools must, for example, pursue a path of rigorous scholarship and intellectual development. They must also, however, pursue the equally important path of genuine spiritual transformation. Christian schools must work to equip students who not only possess a sound biblical worldview but who, like the apostle Paul, can also speak confidently into and about the culture in which they live. Our students must move about the world with confidence and yet resist the seductive call of that world. They must engage the world with passion and grace and wisdom and compassion. Schools that accomplish these outcomes will begin to attract the attention of people possessing wealth and influence.

As essential as trust is in building a strong partnership, it is not enough. The other thing I've learned about people of wealth is that they tend to give to advance their own passion, not yours. If you want them to support your school, you must infect them with a passion for your purpose. In other words, your passion must become their passion, and that change takes some effort.

To infect people with your cold isn't difficult. All you have to do is sneeze in their direction a few times. It's a greater challenge, however, to infect someone with an idea or with a cause. You must, however, accept that challenge if you hope to forge the kinds of partnerships that can make a difference at your school. Here are some thoughts on how to proceed—some rules of engagement.

Commit the Time

You are an educator, but you are also an entrepreneur, a leader, and the chief storyteller for your school. To fulfill one of your primary tasks, therefore, you must continually look for audiences, large and small, to whom you can tell the compelling story of your school.

I'm not talking about trying to garner an invitation to speak in a local church. Such an invitation could certainly benefit your school, but an invitation to speak on Christian schooling at a local church rarely takes place.

Building partnerships with local pastors is good, but you must do more. Join the chamber of commerce. Attend its meetings. Identify key business leaders in your community. Invite them to lunch. Take the mayor to lunch. Get out of your office regularly to meet people. Some of the best advice I ever received was simply never to eat lunch alone.

Prepare for Initial Contact

Before you meet with any person for the first time, do your homework. Find out what is important to him or her. Look for common connections by researching the Internet or by reading newspaper articles or business literature. Before you try to infect people with your passion, let them speak of their own passions.

The people you meet with will expect you to talk about what is important to you. Surprise them by seeking to understand who they are and what they think is important. Develop some good questions that are based on what you have learned about them so that they will talk about themselves. In most cases they will soon ask about you, your history, and your passions. Prepare to respond wisely, and note that on occasion people will go right to what they see as the bottom line.

Before you meet with people, carefully prepare a brief bio. Focus on your passion—not your accomplishments. Don't give your standard speech about your school. Stay focused on how your personal passion has led you to where you are. Connect first with their hearts. If you make that connection, you will find a later opportunity to begin speaking on a more intellectual level.

Connect Through a Connector When Possible

Approach the forging of powerful partnerships with key people as a team sport. You need to involve everyone possible—including board members, faculty and staff, friends, family, alumni, parents, and grandparents—to help you with this crucial task. Find people who know you, who view you in a positive light, and who value what your school is doing; but also look for people whom Malcolm Gladwell calls connectors (2002, 38).

Just who are connectors? They are people who know lots of people. Connecting is not, however, just about knowing. Connectors possess a gift. They intuitively and naturally make social connections. They see relationship patterns that most people miss. In fact, they find those patterns fascinating and love to make connections between people they see sharing those patterns (Gladwell 2002, 38).

Connectors are crucial in helping you build powerful partnerships because connectors can and most often will connect you to people who can make a difference. However, connectors will make the connections only if they trust you. Connectors may not possess substantial financial resources, but they usually know people who do. If they trust you and share a passion for your purpose, they will help make the connections.

Be a Winsome Warrior

I believe that you need to take on the role of winsome warrior as the point person in this crucial partnership-building endeavor. In my mind being winsome and being a warrior are complementary qualities. Consider this description of winsomeness from Chuck Swindoll:

> Winsomeness. That tasteful, appealing, ultra-magnetic quality … that charisma … that ability to cause joy and genuine pleasure in the thick of it all. When a teacher has it, students line up for the course. When a dentist or physician has it, his practice stays full. When a salesman has it, he gets writer's cramp filling out orders. When an usher has it, the church is considered friendly. When a college president has it, the public relations department has a downhill slide….

Winsomeness *motivates*. It releases the strangle-hold grip of the daily grind. It takes the sting out of reality. Winsomeness *simplifies*. Things suddenly seem less complicated ... less severe ... less bothersome. The hole at the end of the tunnel becomes far more significant than the dark passage leading to it. Winsomeness *encourages*. Without ignoring the wrong, winsomeness focuses on the benefits, the hopes, the answers. Even when it must deal with jagged disappointment or inescapable negatives, winsomeness stands tall and refuses to spend the night in such dwellings. (1983, 101–2; italics and three-point ellipses in original)

Follow Up

If you don't follow up with people, you expose yourself to the very real risk of becoming, as Keith Ferrazzi puts it, "lost in their mental attic" (2005, 105). Ferrazzi notes, "Good follow-up alone elevates you above 95 percent of your peers" (106). You should take that remarkable assertion very seriously. Within twenty-four hours of any meeting, you should send along a note in which you do the following:

- Express your gratitude to the person for investing the time in meeting with you
- Include something of interest from your conversation
- Reaffirm any commitments you both made
- Tell the person you look forward to meeting again in the future

In the age of e-mails, Twitter, and messaging, you might be asking about the best means of follow-up. I admit I approach this question with a bit of a bias. I don't think it is wrong to follow up through e-mail. Messaging might even make sense in some situations. I think you follow up best, however, through a handwritten note on attractive stationery. E-mails are a dime a dozen, but a handwritten note is rare. Because of its rarity, it makes a much greater impact.

Consider one final thought on follow-up. Send an additional follow-up note, this one to the gatekeeper. Every busy person has one. You need to make the gatekeeper your ally. If you treat that person like the invisible man or woman, you are making a huge mistake. And doing so is simply wrong. As Francis Schaeffer once noted, "There are no little people" (1974, 21).

Get to know the names of the gatekeepers. Take the time to talk with them. Don't just treat them as conduits to the people you have arranged to meet. Ask them questions. Remark on the pictures on their desks. Find out how long they have been in their current positions. Often you'll learn crucial facts through casual conversation. Always greet them warmly and always thank them for their help.

Stay in Touch

As Keith Ferrazzi observes, "These days we're overwhelmed with so much information that our minds can prioritize only the most recent data. What does it take to break through the white noise of information overload? Becoming front and center in someone's mental Rolodex is contingent on one invaluable concept: repetition" (2005, 181–182). Staying in touch means a phone call, an e-mail, or a note at least once a month. If you want to take your relationship to a deeper level, to the partnership level, you will need to meet with that person face-to-face outside the office at least a couple of times a year. Also remember birthdays and other important events. And when you send a card, make it personal. If you want to catch someone's attention, include a note; otherwise, that person may well assume you are just going through the motions.

My supporters live all over the country, so I can stay in touch most easily through some form of electronic media. I've come to understand, however, that over time the relationship tends to die unless I can find a way for face-to-face meetings. Thus I try to connect with my supporters whenever my travels take me anywhere near them. Nothing replaces a hug or a warm handshake. The power of a shared meal, a good conversation, and laughter is hard to overestimate.

Make It a True Partnership

A shared meal and quality conversation may strengthen a partnership, but a true partnership requires all the partners to invest resources in the common purpose. Your school needs partners to fulfill its mission. If you want partners, be a partner; and what sets a partner apart from a friend is the willingness to make a real investment in the common purpose.

Many people ask about what I do and even encourage me in what I do. Far fewer people invest in what I do. They are my partners. For the partnership to be complete, however, I must invest in their lives as well. If you want to deepen your partnership with other people, tangibly invest in their lives.

A person of wealth who invests in your school does not need your money, but you can certainly invest something in return. Perhaps you can use your expertise, talent, and knowledge to help someone solve a problem. For example, I've used my strategic-planning expertise to help supporters who lead ministries or own businesses.

Find something you can give as an investment in the lives of your partners. I find that something as simple as sending along books or articles is a good way to make that investment. On occasion I have been able to act as a connector for a partner. What you bring to the partnership may vary, but you must invest something if you want to create a true partnership.

Stay on Message

Anyone who knows me knows my passions. I tend to wear my heart on my sleeve. And I don't apologize for being that way. On occasion my wife gently places her hand on my knee to remind me to turn down the intensity, a reminder that is most certainly good, but to know me is to know my heart.

All of us have heard the advice to avoid discussions of religion or politics at parties or family gatherings. I suggest that conversations about Christian schooling sometimes generate nearly as much heat. That is one of the reasons many pastors avoid the topic. As a Christian school leader, however, you can't avoid the topic. Be winsome, be gracious, but don't be afraid to speak of your passion.

Allow me a word of caution, however. You don't want to become a Johnny-one-note who bores people to death. Since boring people to death in no way builds relationships or partnerships, we all need to broaden our interests. Read broadly so that you can add value to all kinds of conversations. When people discuss various topics, think of yourself as the supporting cast, not the main character. Learn to add spice to conversations, but not so much that you overwhelm the flavor.

If you want to infect others with your passion, keep delivering your message. Keep looking for interesting ways to voice your message, but stay on message. Nothing is quite so powerful as a compelling story well told.

Chapter Thirteen
The Underground Stream

Let me make an admission. I have passion for the topic of planned giving, and I know I want to help your school become financially strong. I also recognize, however, how much more I need to know about planned giving. Although it is not my area of expertise, I believe that you as a school leader must learn about it. Thus this chapter is intended as an introduction to a subject you simply cannot ignore and about which you must be willing to learn more.

Think of income from planned giving as an underground stream feeding all three areas of your budget: operations, program enhancements, and capital projects. In addition, revenue from planned giving can significantly boost your scholarship fund, allowing you to make your school accessible to all area families who understand the value of quality Christian schooling and who desire that schooling.

Despite huge losses resulting from one of the most serious economic downturns in U.S. history, an enormous amount of wealth still resides in the pocketbooks of many people in the United States. Before the crash of 2008, predictions existed that the builder and boomer generations would transfer about $40 trillion of private wealth to their children and grandchildren (*Insurance Journal* 2004). Even if that wealth has declined 30 percent, almost $30 trillion in wealth will transfer over the next twenty years or so.

That is a lot of money. But Christian schools, which for the most part have done a poor job in all areas of resource development, are especially lagging in planned giving. I don't have access to any valid research numbers regarding Christian schools and planned giving, so someone might be motivated to call me on my assertion, but here is what I do know.

In more than thirty presentations of my Strategic Finance enabler presented on behalf of ACSI, I addressed over 1,000 school leaders and board members. In each of those presentations, I asked this question: How many of you have an endowment of at least $1 million? Of all the schools represented by those hundreds of leaders, only one had such an endowment. I suspect that more ACSI-affiliated schools can now claim an endowment in excess of $1 million; I also suspect that the number is still low—probably very low. That fact must change, or I believe more schools will find themselves at risk.

Basic Questions About Planned Giving

So what can you do? You can begin by thinking through the following nine questions.

1. What is planned giving?
2. What is the biblical foundation for planned giving?
3. What keeps us from talking to people about planned giving?
4. What motivates people to give planned gifts?
5. Why would someone give a planned gift to you?
6. What keeps people from giving planned gifts?
7. What is your responsibility to those who give planned gifts?
8. What are some typical misconceptions about planned giving?
9. What are some initial steps?

Question 1: What Is Planned Giving?

In *Planned Giving Simplified*, Robert F. Sharpe, Sr. writes, "Planned giving is people (givers) doing what they want to do with their assets and gift planners helping them do it" (1999, xxi). That statement uses pretty simple language to describe something that can, because of state and federal tax laws, be quite complex.

Obviously you will find a bit more to consider, as Sharpe acknowledges:

Making a gift is an act of voluntarily transferring something one possesses to another without expecting anything in return. The gift becomes a tax-deductible charitable gift when it is delivered to a qualified tax-exempt institution. People make either planned or unplanned charitable gifts. Unplanned gifts are made without much thought and are often small. Examples of this can be anything from tossing a dollar in the collection bucket of a street Santa to writing a $100 check after being touched emotionally by a charity's mailing. Planned gifts usually are completed after considerable thought on the part of the donor and are given for any purpose that serves the mission of the organization…. A large gift is whatever the giver considers larger than what they normally give. (1999, 3)

So in one sense, planned giving *is* simple. People choose to make a gift to a specific charitable organization for a specific reason on the basis of a thoughtful process rather than an emotional response. In another sense, planned giving is complicated for at least two reasons. First, tax law is complicated—so complicated that planning giving usually requires the help of a certified professional. Second, personal motivation entails complexity because the reasons motivating a person to make a planned gift to an organization usually run deep in the person's heart and mind.

Gift planning in its basic form also responds to the following three important questions, all of which add a certain layer of complexity to the entire process:
- What gift asset should a donor use—cash, stock, mutual funds, bonds, real estate, family business, antiques, or any number of other sources?
- How should a person structure the gift—outright bequest, trust, deed, contract, bargain sale, donor-advised fund, supporting organization, or some other structure?
- When should the person make the gift—during life or at death?

Is your head beginning to spin? Unless you have some background in planned giving, I suspect it is. And guess what? The topic can become even more complex. But please don't let that reality deter you from pursuing this important component of resource development. Just recognize what you don't know. Then find someone you can trust who can help guide you—someone who has the relevant experience and expertise and who shares your biblical understanding of stewardship.

Question 2: What Is the Biblical Foundation for Planned Giving?

In earlier chapters I have spent considerable time looking at key biblical principles that should shape financial practice in a Christian school. I'm going to add to and perhaps expand on that material a bit here.

Ownership is God's; stewardship is ours. Though I strongly believe in the right of private property, I find it interesting that in the Old Testament all property belonged to Yahweh. The Israelite economy was an interesting hybrid of modern-day capitalism and theocratic ownership. When Israel entered the land of promise, the land was divided among the twelve tribes. Then each portion of that land was further divided among the families in each tribe.

The families could then work the land they had received. If they worked wisely and diligently, they could profit. If they managed their land poorly, they might soon find themselves under contract as laborers to a more successful member of their tribe.

Individual Israelites could use much of their profit for personal reasons, but all Israelites were required to give a series of tithes to support national worship—including support for the Levites, who were given the responsibility for national worship—and to give generously to help those experiencing genuine need. The book of Ruth, for example, gives us a picture of how the law of gleaning helped meet needs.

The key point here is that God gave the Israelites a gift—land. In addition, He gave them the freedom to make wise use of that land to provide for their needs and even desires. Make no mistake, however. It was not their land; it was Yahweh's, as all the laws related to the Year of Jubilee clearly indicate. Private ownership of property as an economic practice is a powerful way to keep a central government from gaining too much control over the lives of its citizens. Unfortunately, private property can breed among us, the followers of Christ, the idea that all we own belongs to us to do with as we desire.

I will stand firmly with those who want to keep the government from taking too great a percentage of private wealth to use as it sees fit. When any government assumes the power to confiscate and redistribute private wealth, it becomes too easy for it to assume control of individual lives beyond the authority the Scriptures clearly give.

I will also, however, stand firmly on the principle that all I own and all you own belongs to God. Thus we have a primary responsibility to exercise wise stewardship over those resources in a manner that reflects God's character and advances God's purposes. (Study Paul's instructions to Timothy on the proper use of wealth: 1 Timothy 6:6–19.)

To fulfill our responsibility with integrity, we need to understand that we have a primary role not just to raise money for our organization. We also have an obligation to help people better understand the full meaning of the lordship of Christ and to encourage them to embrace the call to a life of joyous generosity.

I appreciate the way Todd Harper of Generous Giving puts it: "In fundraising, there is a great temptation to focus solely on the needs of the organization. In order to move beyond fundraising to transformational disciple making, the focus must shift to the needs and interests of others. People are drawn toward those who are free from the need to look out for their own interests and can instead focus on the needs of others" (2008, 227). That is wise, biblical advice.

In one sense we can state the truth this simply: "If God owns it all, then spending money is spending *God's* money, and therefore spending is always a spiritual decision" (Haynie 2008, 81; italics in original). As Douglas John Hall reminds us, "Stewardship is no longer concerned with matters—including religious matters—on the periphery of existence; it belongs to the essence of things. For the call to responsible stewardship encounters us precisely at the heart of our present-day dilemma and impasse" (95).

Question 3: What Keeps Us from Talking to People About Planned Giving?

I think the number one reason we don't talk to people about giving is the personal discomfort most of us feel when talking about money, especially someone else's money. There was a time when I just couldn't imagine asking someone to consider making a gift to an organization or funding a project. I could talk eloquently about giving in the abstract while standing behind a lectern. But put me in a face-to-face situation and I struggled to put two intelligible words together.

I began to look deep inside my heart for an answer. What I discovered was a bit painful. I discovered fear—fear that people would deny my request. I discovered pride; I didn't want to put myself in a position of dependency because it made me feel small and inconsequential. I discovered envy; I found myself upset with God that I didn't have resources similar to those of the people of wealth from whom I was seeking gifts. I discovered more murk and mud, but I think you get the picture.

To decrease personal discomfort, remind yourself that you are simply obeying God's call to let Him use you as an agent of transformation in people's lives. It isn't that the project, program, or organization for which you must find resources is unimportant. No wise steward is going to give to fund something that doesn't make a real difference. Rather, raising money for any project, no matter how important, takes a secondary position to helping people understand more fully the joy of generosity.

I've also discovered that few people are willing to perform a task for which they have not been equipped. Some people can intuitively approach someone and present a request for funding. They need merely minimal preparation. They have a gift. I don't have that gift, and you probably don't either. That fact doesn't, however, relieve you of your responsibility as a leader of the school you serve. If you lack training, you need to seek training. You can find many wonderful resources, some of which you will find in appendix C in the back of this book. Contact them and obtain the training you need.

I hear another cluster of reasons why leaders do not believe they would be using their time in the best way if they spent it asking others to become partners with their school. Let's see if you hear yourself in any of these comments:

- "There is too much going on at our school. I just don't have the time to go out to meet with people."
- "Our school doesn't have the resources that a larger school has. I'm a

one-man/woman shop. When I'm away from the school, there is no one to take charge."
- "We just don't know any wealthy people. It would be a waste of our time."

Left untreated, the "It's just not worth our time" syndrome can be lethal. Please consider this brutal reality. No one else is going to work to advance your school. If you don't engage in building strong partnerships, it won't happen. If it doesn't happen, you put your school at risk. Nothing is more worth the time than sharing your heart about something of inestimable value with people who can, if their hearts are open to God's leading and your mission, make a significant impact on funding your mission.

Question 4: What Motivates People to Give Planned Gifts?

For the most part, people who make planned gifts to an organization have previously made small gifts of some kind. Typically they not only have made initial small gifts but also have begun giving regularly through some kind of annual-fund program. By the way, planned giving, like a capital campaign, will struggle to succeed if your school hasn't already developed a strong annual-fund program.

The motivations behind any gift can be complex. Some people give because they understand their obligation as stewards of God's resources, though I suspect stewardship is still a largely misunderstood concept. Some people give out of a sense of guilt. Others give in response to a particular event. Some give because of tax laws. Some give simply because they have a giving spirit or because people they love and respect have influenced them to do so. Some give because they value the organization or they are moved by what the organization can accomplish. Some give out of a general sense of wanting to give back.

A multitude of factors are working in the heart and mind of every giver, especially when a person is considering a substantial planned gift or a major gift to a capital project. You thus need to learn as much as you can about the passions that shape the lives and actions of the people whom God sends to be part of your mission. But remember this key: you cannot really understand what is going on in the heart and mind of a giver unless you share his or her joy of giving.

Question 5: Why Would Someone Give a Planned Gift to You?

Quite simply, people will be motivated to make a planned gift to you if the following are true:

- They share a passion for the mission, values, and beliefs of your organization.
- They have confidence in the character and competence of your organization's leadership—that is, of the board, the CSO, and the staff.
- They have confidence in your vision of the future and in your ability to achieve that vision.
- They can see the difference you have made and can make in their lives, in the lives of their family (especially their children or grandchildren), in the lives of their friends, in the church, in the community, and in the world. That impact must be both visible and meaningful.
- You ask.

As I've mentioned, the greatest challenge the Christian school movement faces is that people simply do not see the value of what we do. To most people, Christian education is a nice alternative, not a necessary responsibility. Every Christian school leader must set the goal of challenging and changing the way the average believer in the United States views the purpose and potentially powerful impact of Christian schooling.

Question 6: What Keeps People from Giving Planned Gifts?

People don't give for some simple reasons:

- No one ever asks them.
- No one has properly taught them about giving.
- They fear losing their economic freedom as a result of unexpected emergencies, inadequate assets to care for a surviving spouse, an unexpected disability, or inadequate savings for an extended retirement.
- They desire to leave an inheritance to their descendants.

No one other than you and your team can address the first issue. No one else will, on your behalf, engage in conversations related to planned giving. You will certainly benefit from wise counsel, quality coaching, and occasional help from a qualified planned-giving consultant in making a presentation. Because of a unique situation, it might make sense at some point to have someone make a presentation on your behalf, but that occasion should be rare.

It has been my experience that people of wealth will want to talk to an organization's chief spokesperson. They want to take the measure of that person. Remember, their giving depends to a large degree on the answers to two questions: Do they trust you? and Do they believe in what you are doing? Who better for them to meet than the person entrusted with leading the organization? Who better to make the case for the mission of the organization? Who better to explain how their gifts will help the organization better fulfill that mission? Delegate that responsibility to someone else (unless that someone else has a strong personal relationship with the donor), and you will send a powerfully negative message.

In comparison, the final two issues present more of a challenge. No biblically sound ministry leader or planned-giving consultant would ever pressure a donor into making a planned gift that would put that person at risk. A prime reason that God gives us wealth is to provide for our families, including when necessary our extended families. The apostle Paul deals with this admonition when writing the letter we looked at earlier in this chapter: "If anyone does not provide for his own, and especially for those of his household, he has denied the faith and is worse than an unbeliever" (1 Timothy 5:8, NASB). These are powerful but clear words.

We could debate, almost endlessly I suspect, what it means to provide for someone's family. Some people see providing for their families as ensuring several really nice vacations every year. Others have somewhat lower expectations. In both cases, however, it is appropriate to accept responsibility for planning ahead to ensure that one has enough resources available beyond the time of retirement. That reality is one of the reasons planned giving is called planned giving.

I believe that planned giving takes place most effectively in the context of estate planning during which a couple or a person thinks about how best to exercise biblical stewardship. No foolproof plans exist, but planning is always better than simply waiting for a forced decision.

As to the final point, you must always be sensitive to the desires of any donor. Some people work an entire lifetime with the goal of leaving a large estate to their children. I'm not sure that goal is biblical or wise, but I know how powerfully it can motivate people. The key here is to understand that most people capable of leaving a planned gift will want to give part of their estate to their children or grandchildren. You should not try to talk them out of that desire. Most people experience the estate-planning process as a teaching time. You must take great care, however, to best respond to each person's desires.

Question 7: What Is Your Responsibility to Those Who Give Planned Gifts?

Ron Blue, the president of Kingdom Advisors, describes the role of a financial advisor with three words: *advisor, leader,* and *counselor* (2008, 350). Pay careful heed to his description of each of these roles.

Advisor

> Our responsibility is to facilitate the decision-making process, taking into account where clients fall on the spectrum of spirituality, and encourage implementation, which contributes to the client's peace of mind. Obviously one of the prerequisites for this role is technical competence. Our clients come because they need advice regarding their finances, so the most obvious response is to educate them about their financial options. The difference is that we are able to go beyond professional expertise and integrate biblical principles, even for those who want nothing to do with Christ. (Blue 2008, 350)

Note the emphasis of focusing on the person's comfort—a ministry task—rather than simply building a portfolio. Note as well the focus on professional competence. Being competent is ministry as well. You must possess character and competence.

Leader

> Some of the decisions we challenge our clients to make as they seek to become conformed to the image of Christ are difficult ones, and they likely will not walk down those paths without a bit of friendly encouragement and solid examples of mature stewardship and generosity. Our role is to live in such a way as to be able to tell our clients, as Paul told the Corinthian church, "Be imitators of me, as I am of Christ." (Blue 2008, 351)

Again note the emphasis. You can never ask someone to do something you yourself have not been willing to do, even if that something is fully biblical. First of all, to do so is not honest. Second, people will rarely follow you to a place you have not been. If you do not generously give, if you have not made careful plans about your financial future, you will find it hard to encourage others to do so.

Counselor

As a counselor our primary purpose is to remove barriers by engaging our clients in dialogue. It overlaps with the role of advisor because it encourages us to speak the language of our client. Viewing ourselves as counselors reminds us that a memorized script is not enough. Individuals understand issues from radically diverse perspectives that reflect their unique experiences, and our job is to adapt our words so that our meaning and care are evident. (Blue 2008, 352)

You need to listen with care. You need to discern the reality behind the words. You need to gently separate reality from perception. Peeling back the accumulated layers of tangled emotions and fragile relationships isn't easy, but sometimes you, as a good counselor, must help people do that peeling. Until the heart is clear of emotional debris, the mind will find it hard to make wise decisions.

You must do more than just listen, however. You also need to give wise counsel. Sometimes a well-constructed question will nudge a person in the right direction. But on occasion people need a bit more direction. Remember that people bring not only emotion to the planning conversation but also presuppositions, beliefs, and assumptions. So you may need to nudge a bit harder.

You can often start effectively by asking questions beginning with such phrases as "have you ever considered?" It makes sense, as well, to encourage people to read through, for example, Randy Alcorn's *The Treasure Principle* (2001) or another good, brief survey of a biblical approach to giving. In the end, however, most people will make decisions about planned giving on the basis of some internal frame of reference, and they—not you or me—are, after all, the stewards God will hold accountable for those decisions.

In all those roles—advisor, leader, and counselor—we have two additional responsibilities. First, we must act in every way with absolute integrity. At no time must we place our desires before the desires of the person making a planned gift. Second, we must do all we do with exceptional quality and service. In planned giving, there is no place for half measures or incompetence.

Question 8: What Are Some Typical Misconceptions About Planned Giving?

Misconception 1: Planned giving will hurt capital-fund and annual-fund efforts

People making planned gifts do so for a variety of reasons that are usually intensely personal and driven by their own passion. Some people might give planned gifts in the context of a specific capital project, but most people give to advance an organization's overall mission or to fund a particular project of interest. Giving attention to a donor's personal passion typically yields both current and deferred gifts, neither at the other's expense.

Misconception 2: Planned giving takes too long to benefit the organization

In some cases people give gifts in such a narrow way that their impact on an organization becomes increasingly negligible over time, but that outcome rarely occurs when donors receive excellent assistance from godly, competent estate planners. Typically people who give gifts to ministry organizations through a quality gift-planning process have made a commitment to the future. They give because they have confidence in the current leadership and share the mission, values, and vision of the organization. They see the organization's real-time impact, and they view their gifts as a way to ensure that those benefits continue for future generations.

Most long-term givers to any organization tend to layer their gifts. By *layer* I mean that they will continue to support the organization's short-term needs through ongoing annual gifts, but they will give to provide for long-term needs as well. Givers of this kind don't respond well to the culture of crisis that constantly seeks gifts to survive. When you build your annual giving around year-to-year survival, you discourage the very people who can best help build a sustainable financial future for your school.

Misconception 3: Gift planning is too complex for us

Undoubtedly gift planning is the most challenging, complicated part of resource development. In fact, you should not plunge into gift planning until you find someone you can trust who possesses the requisite knowledge, experience, and expertise. You do need help, but you can find quality help.

Do your homework. Put together a profile of the kind of person you are looking for who will give you help. If you are unsure of how to build such a profile or of how to begin looking, contact someone you trust who has been involved in planned giving. Ask for help. Don't put off your request because of fear. Remember this: wise stewards seeking to make a gift to any organization will demand help from skilled professionals who have a track record of integrity, biblical wisdom, and success in estate planning. Find the best or don't engage, because choosing poorly will most certainly yield negative long-term consequences.

Misconception 4: We cannot afford planned giving

Here's my question for anyone who believes that. If between $20 and $40 trillion dollars will pass from one generation to the next over the next twenty to thirty years, what portion of that money are you willing to ignore? If you want to be serving your community in ten, fifteen, or twenty years, and if tuition rates are already a barrier to many parents, where will you find the necessary funding? I may be wrong, though I don't think I am: you simply cannot afford to ignore this opportunity.

Question 9: What Are Some Initial Steps?

To begin, deepen and broaden your own understanding. Contact Generous Giving, Crown Financial Ministries, Good Sense, Kingdom Advisors, or the Evangelical Council for Financial Accountability and ask for information on planned giving. You will also probably find the names of some quality, well-vetted planned-giving professionals who live in your area. In addition, you may want to read the *Chronicle of Philanthropy*, another excellent source of current practice. You will find contact information for these organizations in Appendix C.

You do not need to set the goal of becoming a planned-giving expert. You do need, however, to become conversant with the language and practices of planned giving to the extent that you can develop a nose for trouble. The world of investment, estate planning, and gift planning tends to attract charlatans, and people making end-of-life decisions can be vulnerable. You need to play gatekeeper. To fulfill that responsibility, you simply must learn as much as possible.

Once you have gained some understanding of planned giving, begin educating your constituents. As I mentioned, you could probably educate your constituents in concert with other area Christian schools as well as with local churches. A workshop featuring a planned-giving expert associated with a well-known national organization and cosponsored by a wide array of area ministries will more readily attract attention than something sponsored by a single church or school.

Such cooperative efforts rarely occur, however. I suspect that ministry leaders, including pastors and school administrators, fear losing gifts to another ministry. I suppose such a loss may occur, but the possibility is remote at best. A person able and willing to make a substantial planned gift will almost always make that gift for all the reasons we explored earlier.

Conclusion

My great-aunts never lived in a house that had running water. They had the old-fashioned well I previously described, and I now realize something about that well. It was never the source of the water. It was only the means of accessing the water already there. On the surface the Hill Country of Texas is a pretty dry place. Underground, however, is a different story. Seams of limestone capture, filter, and store large quantities of rainwater. There the water waits until someone comes along and digs a well. Then and only then does the ground give up its life-giving treasure.

God provides enormous resources—like those reservoirs of water waiting to be tapped—to fund His purposes in the world. You can find some of those resources on the surface. Many of them, however, remain out of sight—beneath the ground, so to speak. You can do the work of digging a well, or you can ignore that rich source and continue to haul water from a distant source. The choice is largely up to you. The task does not lie beyond your ability, but it will require some hard work, and it does bring a bit of risk. You can gain the reward, however, of a deep, continually flowing source of the financial resources you need to fund your mission and vision.

Chapter Fourteen
What Now?

When I first started the research for the seminar upon which this book is based, I brought to that research a certain set of assumptions. As I stated in the first chapter, I saw weak finances as the greatest threat to an individual Christian school and to the Christian school movement as a whole. I must confess that as I come to the end of this project (which now extends over five years) my thinking has changed a bit.

I still believe that weak finances are a threat to Christian schools. But I now see finances as a threat in the way a high fever can be a threat to your personal health. Left unchecked for a long enough period of time, a high fever can cause serious damage to the body, even leading to death in severe cases. A school cannot endure prolonged periods of financial instability and weaknesses any more than a body can endure prolonged periods of elevated temperatures.

A fever, however, is what we would call a presenting problem. In other words, it is a symptom of an underlying problem that must be diagnosed and then treated if the fever is to be eliminated. That problem can be an infection of some sort, or it could signal that the body is at war with itself as it fights some kind of cancer. Taking aspirin or lying in a tub of cold water can reduce the severity of the fever for a period of time, but until the underlying problem is addressed, anything you do will provide only temporary relief, leaving the real problem to continue its assault against the body.

That is what I have come to realize about the financial struggles faced by most schools. I had a sense of this as I entered into this project, and that is why I have placed such an emphasis on the integrated nature of creating and maintaining the fiscal health of any school. As I draw this book to a conclusion, I want to briefly—very briefly because of space limitations—identify what I see as the real underlying causes for the financial struggles of so many Christian schools.

Speaking the Truth in Love

Speaking the truth in love is a remarkably difficult thing to do, partly because we know that in doing so we risk damaging a relationship and partly because all of us are blind to certain realities about ourselves. In this I'm no different than anyone reading this book. There are things about me that I might suspect are true, but I'm not sure I'm always ready to hear those things from someone else. Now it helps if I know that the other person has my best interest at heart, but even then it can be painful.

The fact is that I don't know most of you who have chosen to purchase and read this book. I am grateful that you have done so, and I hope you have found the investment of time and money to be worthwhile. But even though I may not know you personally, my goal from the first day I tapped out the first word of this book has been simple: I want to help you become all that God has called you to be as a leader of a Christian school.

I have experienced firsthand the challenges inherent in leading a Christian school. During all my years as head of school, there was never a time when I did not feel the enormous weight of the budget, never a time when I didn't struggle with the salaries we were paying our faculty and staff, never a time when I didn't wonder how much better a school we could be if we just had a few extra dollars to spend on materials or facilities or equipment or any number of other crucial needs. So as I make some concluding observations, please understand that what I have to say is driven by my passion to help you fulfill your calling with excellence.

So, if struggling financially is more symptom than problem, what are the problems? In answering that question I am not going to rely on "the research." I won't do that for two simple reasons. First of all, I am not aware of any real research on this topic. Second, I am honestly not all that enamored with sociological research. I learned to be skeptical of "the research" while in graduate school;

not much since then has raised my level of confidence. So in the absence of real research I am going to share some significant anecdotal observations of my own.

As I have observed schools across the country for many years, as I have engaged in countless conversations with school leaders and have read everything I can find on related topics, I have come to conclude that there are three primary issues that often have a negative impact on the fiscal health of a school. Not all schools struggle at the same level. Not all struggle continually. But it is the rare school that doesn't face difficulty in one of these three areas at one time or another.

1. The first problem is our ongoing failure to make a clear, compelling case for Christian schooling. We simply haven't grabbed the hearts, minds, and imaginations of enough of those people who should be our key constituency.
2. The second contributing problem, sad to say, is mediocre performance in delivering our educational mission and providing quality customer service.
3. The third is the most important: it is inadequate leadership at the building level as well as on the board.

Have I upset you yet? As you ponder that brief list, what is your reaction? I suspect that most of you have gone into defensive mode. That is normal. That is certainly what I would do. And the fact of the matter is I could be wrong. I don't have the benefit of divine revelations or, as I said, "the research." But I would encourage you to at least consider my observations.

A Clear, Compelling Case

I just don't think most people—speaking of potential or even current parents, pastors, or community leaders—get what it means to be a Christian school. We (those of us on the inside) think we get it, but I'm not sure even we do. *Christian* as a modifier before the word *school* has come to mean so many things to so many people that it has lost any real defining power. Just what is it that makes a school Christian, and why should that matter to anyone?

Are we a Christian school because we hire only Christian teachers, use Christian-themed textbooks, have Bible classes every day and chapel once a week? Are we a Christian school because we have a statement of faith, espouse a Christian worldview (whatever that means), or require our parents to acknowledge a relationship with Jesus Christ?

As a follower of Jesus Christ, would I use a different kind of instructional strategy than someone who is a follower of John Dewey? If so, why? Are the assured results of "the research" all that matters, or are there other principles that should shape how we approach the classroom? How do we evaluate all that research on teaching and learning that from year to year and study to study seems so often to contradict itself? How will we employ technology? Does it matter? Is the pragmatic answer always the right answer? I wonder, for example, how many really thoughtful conversations were prompted by Donovan Graham's book *Teaching Redemptively* or James K. A. Smith's book *Desiring the Kingdom*. Maybe dozens, or even hundreds—but I wonder.

I'm just not sure that we have truly identified what it means to be a school that approaches its educational mission from a thoroughly Christian perspective or effectively figured out how to communicate that message in such a way that it clearly sets us apart in the marketplace.

Disagree? I'm OK with that. But ask yourself this question: What would happen to the enrollment at your school if an aggregate of just 20 percent of the families with school-aged children who attend local evangelical churches decided to enroll their children at your school next year? Would your enrollment increase or decrease? By how much? Talk to any person whose job involves marketing a product or service, and I suspect they will agree with the following statement: You succeed or fail in your primary marketplace. So what is, or at least should be, your primary marketplace? I would think it would be the families who attend the evangelical churches in your area. If they are not "buying" what you are "selling," then why not? Thoughtfully consider the second issue on my list of three.

Perception and Reputation

Curious as to why such a small percentage of evangelical families consider a Christian college or university as a higher education option for their children, the Council for Christian Colleges and Universities (think ACSI for Christian higher education) commissioned a research study in the mid 1990s to find an explanation.

What they discovered probably has application to the K–12 Christian school movement. Our stock answer to why parents don't choose a Christian school or college is lack of money. When considering where to educate their children, financial considerations are always a part of the decision for parents. The research, however, was pretty clear. The number one factor influencing a parent's decision about higher education choice was not money. It was the perceived *quality of education* at a particular school.

Now some Christian colleges such as Wheaton or Calvin or Westmont—and there are a number of others—have universally positive reputations. When lumped together as a whole, however, most evangelicals had serious concerns about the quality of education their children might receive at a school with a fundamentally religious orientation. And it isn't just perception. While people do tend to paint, as we say, with too broad a brush, it's pretty rare that we hear of an evangelical Christian college or university spoken of in the same way as, say, Notre Dame, Harvard, or Stanford.

It can be a matter of perceived or real limits to key programs, inadequate or worn academic facilities, thin faculty resumes, overextended faculty teaching too many key courses, poor career placement programs, or ... or ... or. Those are realities in many places. Persuading parents to invest $20,000, $25,000, $30,000, or more in the education of their child when they perceive serious inadequacies is a challenge. Fewer and fewer are willing to make that kind of investment to "keep their kids safe."

They realize that the world of business has become incredibly competitive, and they want their children well prepared. As for the spiritual part of their lives, well there is always InterVarsity Christian Fellowship or Cru (formerly Campus Crusade for Christ) or the Baptist Student Union or any number of local churches. You might disagree with that kind of thinking, but it certainly appears to be a significant part of the decision-making process in the typical evangelical home. As Steven Garber observes in his book *The Fabric of Faithfulness*, most evangelical parents, as do most Americans, view education as "the passport to privilege" (1996). In their minds, education is a means to an end—the end being a good job generating a good income that allows for a quality lifestyle.

That is part of the challenge we face in communicating a compelling case. But a compelling case without compelling, unmistakable evidence in support of the case is not likely to have much of an impact. People not only need to believe that what you do is essential in the lives of their students, but they also need to believe that you deliver your mission with excellence. And in the case of Christian schooling, both the spiritual and academic missions must be *perceived* as excellent, or your enrollment will struggle and your inability to attract significant donors will continue—both of which will have significant impact on your fiscal health.

The motivations of your parents will vary from family to family. Some will be attracted more by one thing than another. But I think I can say this with a high degree of confidence: If parents come to the place where they don't believe you are doing a good job at teaching their child to read or compute or write, they are going to remove their child from your school. They may applaud the fact that you love their child. They may thank you for the spiritual impact you have made in the life of their child. But they won't keep their child in your school once they become convinced that the education they are receiving is inadequate.

Does Everything Really Rise or Fall on Leadership?

This is a huge question, way beyond the scope of the few paragraphs I will invest at this time. But the question does capture the essence of my third issue. Here is what I believe after observing a lot of churches, parachurch ministries, and Christian schools over the years: I've never seen sustained excellence in any organization where there is not quality leadership at the top. Charisma is not leadership. Faithfulness and hard work, while important, aren't leadership. Intelligence alone isn't sufficient, nor is proven ability in the classroom. Indeed, in my opinion, much of how we define leadership in the Christian world isn't truly leadership.

I know I may be stepping on some pretty big toes when I make that observation. But I believe it with all my heart. Leadership requires all the following qualities in abundance:

- Character—the person you are, how you respond to the whole gamut of life experiences. Words like *courage, discipline, integrity, persistence, grace, faithfulness,* and *determination* come to mind.
- Knowledge, which encompasses both necessary content and significant, helpful experience.
- Skills to put that knowledge to work in a useful way. It is hard to provide sound fiscal leadership for your school, for example, if you know little or nothing about budgeting and management.
- Wisdom and insight, the ability to consistently apply what you have learned to new situations in a way that accurately reflects your mission and helps you achieve that mission with excellence.
- Talent—those gifts given to you by a sovereign God that allow you to effectively fulfill those specific roles that only a leader can play in an organization.

I'm pretty certain that most of you agree with the first four qualities. I suspect many of you might wonder about that last quality. That is where I find myself in disagreement with much of the literature on leadership. Most books focus on skills or knowledge or character. Learn this information, hone these skills, be this kind of person, and you'll be OK in whatever leadership situation you find yourself. If it were that easy, we'd be overrun with leaders. But we're not. Why do you think that is? Character is central to who we say we are as followers of Jesus Christ. We're all educators and should be able to speak knowingly on any topic related to education. So what is missing? Finding people of character isn't hard. Nor is it all that difficult to find good teachers. So why aren't really high-quality school leaders easier to find?

Once again I am asking a question way beyond the scope of this brief discussion. It is, however, a question upon which we must begin focusing a lot more attention and energy if we ever hope to fully address the struggles we are facing in the Christian school movement. I'm convinced we need to make this our number one objective over the next ten years—a kind of "let's put a man on the moon before the end of this decade" kind of emphasis.

None of that will matter, in my opinion, however, unless we also address the issue of school boards. I must confess that I often wonder if when Jesus talked about "the blind leading the blind" He wasn't thinking of the typical Christian school board. The problems we have in school leadership are real. The problem with school boards is, in my observation, worse. At least we have some certification requirements for teachers and school leaders. For boards there is next to nothing offered and even less expected. Yet how often are poorly equipped boards, with little professional development, given the responsibility for making policy and for ensuring that the head of school performs at a high level that is consistent with the stated mission, core values, and desired outcomes of our schools?

The best I can say about the situation is that it is a pretty mixed bag. Most boards are filled with well-meaning people who, while they may care deeply, are ill-equipped for the job. That is a recipe for continuing frustration, bad decisions, leadership turnover, unhappy staff and parents, and—in far too many cases—closed doors.

I firmly believe that the fiscal health of a school will in large part be determined by how the leadership of that school responds to the stated mission, core values, and desired outcomes of the school. Neglect any, and your school is likely to suffer. You can do a masterful job of managing your budget, but if your enrollment continues to decline it won't matter because you'll soon reach a point at which you won't have enough money to manage. This isn't an either/or scenario. All of the issues I have discussed in this book are crucial; none can be ignored.

The good news is this. It can be done. None of this is all that hard to understand or difficult to implement. You may have to reconsider some of your current practices, challenge some of your cherished beliefs, and stretch your comfort level a bit, but you can be a healthy Christian school that pursues its mission with excellence.

A Concluding Thought

I love this quote from Andy Stanley. In his book *The Next Generation Leader*, he observes, "You may be good. You may even be better than anyone else. But without a coach you will never be as good as you could be" (2003, 12). I couldn't agree more. Over the years I have benefitted repeatedly from the insights and ideas of people more experienced and more gifted than I. I am forever grateful for what I've learned from Bruce Lockerbie. He ignited my passion for this thing called Christian education in a way no one else had, helped me better understand what Christian education is really all about, and then shared ideas with me on how to pursue that passion with excellence.

Whenever I was facing a crucial conversation, had to write a tough report, or challenge the thinking of a particular person of influence within a school or ministry organization, I learned (after some rather painful experiences) to call my good friend Ron Hayden. Ron could take my thoughts and express them so much better and keep me from unnecessarily alienating people by my poor use of language. When he died two years ago, I lost a remarkable coach.

I've had dozens of insightful conversations with my good friend Mickey Bowdon about how best to help schools and school leaders when it comes to planning and decision making. I earned a doctorate in organizational leadership and spent years studying the best in the business. I learned a lot. But Mickey has helped improve my thinking, and he continues to do that even today every time we get the chance to break bread together.

When it comes to business, Roger Humpton, my dear friend and chairman of The Barnabas Group, has been of such great assistance. Our relationship began many years ago when he approached me and asked me to disciple him. I was a young pastor and he was an even younger business owner in our church. I had no clue about actually discipling anyone. He was my guinea pig; I ended up learning more from him than he ever did from me. I still do. He is not only a wise counselor but a dear friend.

I could go on and on. The list is long, going back to my high school years. There were Lynn and Janet Warner, our youth leaders at New Testament Baptist Church in Miami, Florida. There were Verle and Lucille Ackerman, who took me under their wing when my mom and dad got divorced. In college there was Dr. Don Davis, a professor at Baptist Bible College, and Ed Stewart, another professor and the music director at our church, with whom I often clashed but from whom I learned so much.

Currently I have been engaged in an ongoing dialogue with Jan Stump, who for many years served as director of development at a Christian school in Alaska and then for a number of years served on the staff of ACSI leading development and marketing efforts. She has helped me sharpen my thinking on how best to define and articulate this thing we call Christian schooling.

Of course, and most importantly, there is my wife, Linda, who has loved me and tolerated me and challenged me for over forty years now. She made it possible for me to pursue my sometimes crazy ideas and stood with me through some rather challenging times—always encouraging, always steadfast in her faith.

I think you get the picture. Some people have touched me from a distance through their writing, some up close and personal, but only because I invited them into my life and let them influence me. Andy Stanley is right. Who has been your coach? Who influences you today? To whom do you turn when you need some additional insight or wisdom? If there is no one, then I fear you are in grave danger.

From the beginning it was my intent to act as a coach in writing this book. I've tried to be honest in my observations, helpful in my suggestions, and fresh in my thinking. Hopefully you have found benefit as you have read through each chapter. Please feel free to challenge my assumptions and conclusions. As I said earlier, I don't have the benefit of divine revelations. At the same time I hope that you will carefully consider what I've said. The need for quality Christian schools has never been greater. We can ill afford to squander the opportunities we have to make an impact on the lives of young men and women.

Years ago I discovered this quote from the pen of Erasmus of Rotterdam (1466–1536). I'd like to share it with you and pray that it will encourage you as much as it has encouraged me over the years.

> To be a schoolmaster is next to being a king. Do you count it mean employment to imbue the minds of young people with the love of Christ and the best of literature and to return them to their country honest and virtuous men? In the opinion of fools it is a humble task, but in fact it is the noblest of occupations (cited in Lockerbie 1989, 93).

Indeed, it is the noblest of occupations. What an honor. What a responsibility. What a joy.

Appendix A
Resources for Board Leadership

Andringa, Robert C., and Ted W. Engstrom. 1997. *Nonprofit board answer book: Practical guidelines for board members and chief executives*. Washington, DC: National Center for Nonprofit Boards.

Board Source. 2005. *The source: Twelve principles of governance that power exceptional boards*. Washington, DC: Board Source.

Carver, John. 1997. *Boards that make a difference: A new design for leadership in nonprofit and public organizations*. San Francisco, CA: Jossey-Bass.

———. 1997. *Planning better board meetings*. San Francisco, CA: Jossey-Bass.

Carver, John, and Miriam Mayhew Carver. 1996. *Basic principles of policy governance*. San Francisco, CA: Jossey-Bass.

———. 1996. *Your roles and responsibilities as a board member*. San Francisco, CA: Jossey-Bass.

———. 1997. *Reinventing your board: A step-by-step guide to implementing policy governance*. San Francisco, CA: Jossey-Bass.

De Pree, Max. 2001. *Called to serve: Creating and nurturing the effective volunteer board*. Grand Rapids, MI: Eerdmans.

Keenan, Derek J., ed. 2007. *Christian school board governance: A framework for effectiveness*. Colorado Springs, CO: Purposeful Design.

Lowrie, Roy W., Jr, and Roy L. Lowrie. 2004. *Serving God on the Christian school board*. 3rd ed. Colorado Springs, CO: Purposeful Design.

Appendix B
Resources for Stewardship and Resource Development

Books

Ahern, Thomas. 2008. *How to write fundraising materials that raise more money.* Medfield, MA: Emerson and Church Publishers.

———. 2009. *Seeing through a donor's eyes: How to make a persuasive case for everything from your annual drive to your planned giving program to your capital campaign.* Medfield, MA: Emerson and Church Publishers.

Alcorn, Randy. 2001. *The treasure principle: Unlocking the secret of joyful giving.* Sisters, OR: Multnomah.

———. 2003. *Money, possessions, and eternity.* Wheaton, IL: Tyndale House.

Axelrod, Terry. 2002. *Raising more money: A step-by-step guide to building lifelong donors.* Seattle, WA: Raising More Money Publications.

———. 2003. *The point of entry handbook.* Seattle, WA: Raising More Money Publications.

Blomberg, Craig. 2008. *Heart, soul, and money: A Christian view of possessions.* Joplin, MO: College Press.

Brendel, Doug. 1998. *Seven deadly sins of ministry marketing.* Fairlawn, OH: Berkey Brendel Sheline.

Brinkerhoff, Peter C. 1997. *Mission-based marketing.* New York: John Wiley and Sons.

Brown, Larissa Golden, and Martin John Brown. 2001. *Demystifying grant seeking.* San Francisco, CA: Jossey-Bass.

Burk, Penelope. 2004. *Donor centered fundraising*. Chicago, IL: Cygnus Applied Research, Inc.

Colson, Helen A. 2002. *Philanthropy at independent schools*. Washington, DC: NAIS.

DeFrancesco, John, and Gary Goodfriend. 1996. *The common sense guide to publicity*. Chicago, Il: DeFrancesco and Goodfriend Public Relations.

De Pree, Max. 1989. *Leadership is an art*. New York: Dell.

———. 1997. *Leading without power: Finding hope in serving community*. San Francisco, CA: Jossey-Bass.

Dove, Kent E. 1988. *Conducting a successful capital campaign*. San Francisco, CA: Jossey-Bass.

———. 2001. *Conducting a successful development services program*: San Francisco, CA: Jossey-Bass.

Godin, Seth. 2003. *The purple cow*. New York: Penguin Group.

Goodman, Andy. 2002. *Why bad ads happen to good causes*. Santa Monica, CA: Cause Communications.

Grace, Catherine O'Neil, ed. 2001. *Marketing independent schools in the 21st century*. Washington, DC: NAIS.

Grace, Kay Sprinkel, and Alan L. Wendroff. 2001. *High impact philanthropy*. New York: John Wiley and Sons.

Green, Albert E. 1998. *Reclaiming the future of Christian education: A transforming vision*. Colorado Springs, CO: ACSI.

Guiness, Os. 2001. *Doing well and doing good: Money, giving, and caring in a free society*. Colorado Springs, CO: NavPress.

Hanson, Kathleen. 2005. *Student recruitment*. New York: Council for Advancement in Support of Education.

Hughes, Mark. 2005. *Buzzmarketing: Get people to talk about your stuff*. New York: Penguin Group.

Jeavons, Thomas H., and Rebekah Burch Basinger. 2000. *Growing givers' hearts*. San Francisco, CA: Jossey-Bass.

Joyaux, Simone P. 2001. *Strategic fund development: Building profitable relationships*. Gaithersburg, MD: Aspen Publishers.

Lockerbie, D. Bruce. 1996. *From candy sales to committed donors: A guide to financing Christian schools*. Milwaukee, WI: Christian Stewardship Association.

MacArthur, John. 2000. *Whose money is it anyway?* Nashville, TN: Word Publishing.

Matusak, Lorraine. 1997. *Finding your voice*. San Francisco, CA: Jossey-Bass.

Olford, Steven. 1972. *The grace of giving*. Grand Rapids, MI: Baker Books.

Palmer, Parker. 1998. *The courage to teach*. San Francisco, CA: Jossey-Bass.

Panas, Jerold. 1984. *Mega gifts: Who gives them, who gets them*. Chicago, IL: Pluribus Press.

Prince, Russ Alan, and Karen Maru File. 2001. *The seven faces of philanthropy: A new approach to cultivating major donors*. San Francisco, CA: Jossey-Bass.

Ries, Al, and Jack Trout. 1993. *The 22 immutable laws of marketing*. New York: HarperCollins.

Rodin, Scott. 2000. *Stewards in the kingdom: A theology of life in all its fullness*. Downers Grove, IL: InterVarsity.

Seiler, Timothy L. 2001. *Developing your case for support*. San Francisco, CA: Jossey-Bass.

Sharpe, Robert F., Jr. 1999. *Planning giving*. New York: John Wiley and Sons.

Tempel, Eugene, Timothy L. Seiler, and Eva Aldrich, eds. 2011. *Achieving excellence in fundraising*, San Francisco, CA: John Wiley and Sons.

Tybout, Alice M., and Tim Calkins. 2005. *Kellogg on branding*. Hoboken, NJ. John Wiley and Sons.

Wheildon, Colin. 2005. *Type and layout: Are you communicating or just making pretty shapes?* Victoria, Australia: Worsley Press.

Williams, Karla. 1997. *Donor focused strategies for annual giving*. Gaithersburg, MD: Aspen Publishers.

Willmer, Wesley K. 1998. *The prospering parachurch*. San Francisco, CA: Jossey-Bass.

———. 2002. *God and your stuff*. Colorado Springs, CO: NavPress.

———. 2008. *Revolution in generosity: Transforming stewards to be rich toward God*. Chicago, IL: Moody Publishers.

Periodicals

Advancing Philanthropy (AFP), 1101 King Street, Ste 700, Alexandria, VA 22314. www.afpnet.org.

Chronicle of Philanthropy, PO Box 1989, Marion, OH 43306-4089.

Contributions: The How-to Source for Nonprofit Professionals, 508-359-0019. www.contributionsmagazine.com.

Other Resources

AFP: Association of Fundraising Professionals. 703-684-0410; www.afpnet.org.

Benevon. www.benevon.com.

CASE: Council for Advancement and Support of Education. 202-328-5900; www.case.org.

Crown Financial Ministries. www.crown.org.

The Fundraising School: Indiana School of Philanthropy. www.philanthropy.iupui.edu/thefundraisingschool/.

Generous Giving. www.generous giving.org.

Good $ense. www.goodsenseministry.org.

The Good Steward. www.thegoodsteward.org.

Jossey-Bass Publishing. http://www.josseybass.com/WileyCDA/Section/id-2996.html. New York: John Wiley and Sons, Inc.

Maximum Generosity. www.kluth.org.

PRSA: Public Relationship Society of America. www.prsa.org.

Visionresourcing.com. www.visionresourcing.com.

Appendix C
Training Resources for
Planned Giving

Chronicle of Philanthropy. http://philanthropy.com
Crown Financial Ministries. www.crown.org.
Evangelical Council for Financial Accountability. www.ecfa.org.
Generous Giving. www.generousgiving.org.
Good Sense. www.goodsenseministry.com.
Kingdom Advisors. www.kingdomadvisors.org.

References

Alcorn, Randy C. 2001. *The treasure principle: Discovering the secret of joyful giving*. Sisters, OR: Multnomah Publishers.

Barker, Joel Arthur. 1993. *Paradigms: The business of discovering the future*. New York: HarperBusiness.

Beckwith, Harry. 2003. *What clients love: A field guide to growing your business*. New York: Warner Books.

Berry, Jahna. 2011. University of Phoenix enrollment drops 42%. *Arizona Republic*. January 11, 2011. www.azcentral.com/arizonarepublic/business/articles/2011/01/10/20110110university-of-phoenix-enrollment-drops.html.

Blanchard, Ken. 1997. *Mission possible: Becoming a world-class organization while there's still time*. 1997. New York: McGraw-Hill.

Blue, Ronald W. 2008. The financial advisor as an agent of heart transformation. In *Revolution in generosity: Transforming stewards to be rich toward God*, ed. Wesley K. Willmer, 339–358. Chicago, IL: Moody Publishers.

Businessdictionary.com. S.v. "cost center" (by WebFinance). http://www.businessdictionary.com/definition/cost-center.html.

Carver, John, and Miriam Mayhew Carver. 1997. *Reinventing your board: A step-by-step guide to implementing policy governance*. San Francisco, CA: Jossey-Bass.

Collins, James C. 2001. *Good to great: Why some companies make the leap ... and others don't*. New York: HarperCollins Publishers.

Collins, James C., and Jerry I. Porras. 1997. *Built to last: Successful habits of visionary companies*. New York: HarperCollins Publishers.

Council for American Private Education. www.capenet.org/facts.html.

Drucker, P. F. 1969. *The age of discontinuity*. New York: Harper and Row.

————. 2008. *The five most important questions you will ever ask about your organization.* San Francisco, CA: Jossey-Bass.

Eppler, Mark. 2004. *The Wright way: Seven problem solving principles from the Wright brothers that can make your business soar!* New York: AMACOM.

Facilitiesnet.com. 2007. Construction costs continue increase, according to Turner Building Cost Index. September 2007.

Ferrazzi, Keith. 2005. *Never eat alone: And other secrets to success, one relationship at a time.* New York: Currency Books.

Garber, Steven. 1996. *The fabric of faithfulness: Weaving together belief and behavior during the university years.* Downers Grove, IL: InterVarsity Press.

Gladwell, Malcolm. 2002. *The tipping point: How little things can make a big difference.* New York: Back Bay Books.

Gordon, Larry. 2010. College costs increase faster than inflation. *Los Angeles Times*, October 28, 2010.

Graham, Donovan L. 2009. *Teaching redemptively: Bringing grace and truth into your classroom.* 2nd ed. Colorado Springs, CO: Purposeful Design Publications.

Hall, Douglas John. 1990. *The steward.* Grand Rapids, MI: Eerdmans.

Harper, Todd. 2008. Discipleship as a tool to transform hearts toward generosity. In *Revolution in generosity: Transforming stewards to be rich toward God,* ed. Wesley K. Willmer, 223–42. Chicago, IL: Moody Publishers.

Haynie, Richard A. 2008. God and asking: The choice between two roads. In *Revolution in generosity: Transforming stewards to be rich toward God,* ed. Wesley K. Willmer, 79–96. Chicago, IL: Moody Publishers.

Herbert Research. 2005. *Why do Christians not enroll their children in a Christian school?* Belleview, WA: Herbert Research.

Independent School Management. 1997. Your strategic financial plan. *Ideas and Perspectives* 22, no. 5. Independent School Management.

Insurance Journal. 2004. Baby Boomer wealth transfer. www.insurancejournal.com, February 23, 2004.

ISM. See Independent School Management.

Keenan, Derek, comp. ed. 2007. *Christian school board governance: A framework for effectiveness.* 2nd ed. Colorado Springs, CO: Purposeful Design Publications.

Kidner, Derek. 1964. The *Proverbs: An introduction and commentary.* Downers Grove, IL: InterVarsity Press.

Kim, W. Chan, and Renée Mauborgne. 2005. *Blue ocean strategy: How to create uncontested market space and make the competition irrelevant.* Boston, MA: Harvard Business School Publishing.

Kopelman, Josh. 2006. http://redeye.firstround.com.

Lencioni, Patrick. 2002. *The five dysfunctions of a team: A leadership fable.* San Francisco, CA: Jossey-Bass.

Lockerbie, D. Bruce. 1989. *Thinking and acting like a Christian.* Portland, OR: Multnomah.

———. 1996. *From candy sales to committed donors: A guide to financing Christian schools.* Stony Brook, NY: PAIDEIA Press.

McDowell, Josh D. 2006. *The last Christian generation.* Holiday, FL: Greek Key Books.

Mitchell, Mary. 1998. *The first five minutes: How to make a great first impression in any business situation.* With John Corr. New York: John Wiley and Sons.

Money-Zine.com. 2006–2011. Consumer debt statistics.

Peters, Thomas J., and Robert H. Waterman, Jr. 1982. *In search of excellence: Lessons from America's best-run companies.* New York: Warner Books.

Schaeffer, Francis A. 1974. *No little people: Sixteen sermons for the twentieth century.* Downers Grove, IL: InterVarsity.

Sharpe, Robert F., Sr. 1999. *Planned giving simplified: The gift, the giver, and the gift planner.* New York: John Wiley and Sons.

Smith, James K. A. 2009. *Desiring the kingdom: Worship, worldview, and cultural formation.* Grand Rapids, MI: Baker Academic.

Smitherman, Ken. n.d. Four critical issues facing Christian schools. Research summary, Association of Christian Schools International.

Stanley, Andy. 2003. *The next generation leader.* Sisters, OR: Multnomah Publishers.

Swindoll, Charles R. 1983. *Growing strong in the seasons of life.* Portland, OR: Multnomah Press.

Towner, Richard J. 2008. The church's leadership role in bringing stewardship front and center. In *Revolution in generosity: Transforming stewards to be rich toward God,* ed. Wesley K. Willmer, 119–136. Chicago, IL: Moody Publishers.

University of Phoenix. History. www. Phoenix.edu.

Waltke, Bruce K. 2005. *The book of Proverbs: Chapters 15–31.* Grand Rapids, MI: Eerdmans.

Weaver, Richard M. 1948. *Ideas have consequences*. University of Chicago Press. Page references are to the 1984 ed.

Willmer, Wesley K. 2008. *Revolution in generosity: Transforming stewards to be rich toward God*. Chicago, IL: Moody Publishers.